Oakwood's Living History

**FROM THE PROGRESS CLUB
TO A NEW FUTURE — A FAMILY STORY**

"*Oakwood's Living History* tells a compelling story about a country club that has existed for close to 145 years in Kansas City. The book presents a medley of cherished moments, whether it's a memorable round of golf or a beautiful wedding, highlighting its sense of community and Jewish roots. It also focuses on Oakwood's latest iteration — its new facilities, spectacular clubhouse updates, and refurbished golf course."

—Ann Slegman Isenberg, member and freelance journalist

"Ward Katz's history of Oakwood Country Club is an important addition to the many works about the broader history of Kansas City. It speaks to the community at large as much as to the Jews of this region. It is warm, personal, informative, and often quite humorous. What a shame the generations before us do not have the opportunity to enjoy the pleasure of these facts and anecdotes that belonged to them. But how fortunate we, our children, and future readers are to have this delightful book. I was smiling while reading along."

—Randee Krakauer, daughter of Kenneth Krakauer, former club historian and author of When Golf Came to Kansas City

Oakwood's Living History

FROM THE PROGRESS CLUB TO A NEW FUTURE — A FAMILY STORY

By Ward Katz

with Ruth Bigus

MISSION POINT PRESS

Oakwood's Living History

Copyright © 2024 by Ward Katz

All world rights reserved

No part of this book may be reproduced, stored in a retrieval system, or transmitted in any form or by any means electronic, mechanical, photocopying, recording or otherwise, without the prior consent of the publisher.

Readers are encouraged to go to www.MissionPointPress.com to contact the author or to find information on how to buy this book in bulk at a discounted rate.

Published by Mission Point Press
2554 Chandler Rd.
Traverse City, MI 49696
(231) 421-9513
www.MissionPointPress.com

Book design by Sarah Meiers

ISBN 978-1-961302-57-0
Library of Congress Control Number 2024907810

Printed in the United States of America

Dedication

This book is dedicated with love and admiration to my grandparents, Ike and Minnie Katz, and to my parents, Earl and "Sis" Katz. My grandparents' decision to join the Progress Club in 1923 led to over a century of enjoyment for me and my family. My parents were among the lifeblood of Oakwood during that period and we, as a family, spent countless days with them—or with their support—at Oakwood, including Oakwood camp, numerous life cycle events, festive parties, holidays, golf games and just casual dinners. Finally, I dedicate it to the love of my life, Donna, with whom I have shared much of the same.

Table of Contents

Foreword
x

Introduction
ix

CHAPTER 1
The Early Years
—1881 to 1912
1

CHAPTER 2
Expanding Into the Twenties
—1913 to 1929
11

CHAPTER 3
A Challenging Economy
—1930 to 1939
25

CHAPTER 4
The War Years
—1940 to 1949
39

CHAPTER 5
Years of Growth
—1950 to 1959
49

CHAPTER 6
Golf at Oakwood
—The Course
65

CHAPTER 7
A Steady Course Amid
Unsettled Times
—1960 to 1979
73

CHAPTER 8
The Growth Years
—1980 to 1999
89

CHAPTER 9
Oakwood Embraces
a New Future
103

Addendum
123

Oakwood's significant history has earned national recognition.

Foreword

Since 1881, the Progress Club,* and then its successor, Oakwood Country Club, have been integral parts of the Kansas City community. For the thousands of members, guests, friends, and invitees who have come to Oakwood through the years for social, recreational, and business functions as well as marriages and other monumental occasions, it remains a very special place.

For me, starting in my youth through today, Oakwood has been the center of my life and my main source for recreational and social activities. I have made so many friends and worked with so many members who became clients of mine for life—all because of Oakwood.

Ward Katz, a former president of Oakwood, has worked tirelessly with so many of our members to gather pieces of history, photos, and stories to chronicle this amazing story of Oakwood's history in Kansas City. Yes, we turned the page in May 2020 to introduce the "new" Oakwood and its many new amenities to the community. And we have more to do to further improve this jewel, located on one of Kansas City's most beautiful tracts of land.

But cherishing our history will always be important, and this book celebrates that fact. We hope you will appreciate reading and understanding Oakwood's past. We feel it will help you, your family, and your friends treasure this magnificent place even more.

Ken and Lisa Block and Family

The legal name of the club was Progress Club, however, for the purpose of readability it is referred to in this book as "the Progress Club"

INTRODUCTION

This history of Oakwood Country Club is the story of a proud institution that has existed formally for 143 years. There is evidence of its existence in 1879, 145 years ago, but the earliest date of located corporate documents is 1881. Through most of its history, it was widely considered to be a Jewish club and, as such, it is the second longest continuously running organization in the Kansas City Jewish community behind only Congregation B'nai Jehudah.

As discussed in the first chapter, Oakwood (née Progress Club) was started by the leadership of Congregation B'nai Jehudah, largely first or second-generation Reform German Jews seeking a social outlet for themselves and their families. Nearly thirty years after the founding of Progress Club, the automobile had become increasingly available to those with means. Progress Club members sought recreation beyond the urban neighborhoods where they resided. That and the arrival of the game of golf in the Midwest—which intrigued a small number of Progress Club members—resulted in the purchase of a 122-acre farm (actually, an estate) in unincorporated southeast Jackson County, Missouri, from a banker who had fallen on hard times. For purposes of this introduction, I will simply refer to the Progress Club and Oakwood as "the club."

In the mid-1990s, Ken Krakauer, lifetime member and former board member of Oakwood, and national golf historian, wrote a chronological history of the Progress Club and Oakwood. Kenny had also been the editor of the *Oakwoodian* for many years, elevating it to a newsy monthly record of current activity at the club interspersed with historical anecdotes, pictures, records, and newspaper clippings. When I began my term as club president in 1998, Kenny turned the history over to me. He passed away in 2001. Other than its appearance in the program celebrating the 125th anniversary in 2006, the history sat in my files.

TAKE THIS OAKWOOD QUIZ

Oakwood has always been a family club. No area reflects that more than golf. Can you identify the following pairs of relatives who won golf championships at Oakwood?

- Father-Son
- Mother-Son
- Brothers
- Brother-Sister
- Husband-Wife
- Grandmother-Grandchild

Answers are on Page 141.

In or around 2018, when it became apparent that the future of the club, as we knew it, was dubious, I felt a responsibility to update Kenny's document. Having served on the board from 1996 through 2002, I was able to do so based on my involvement in the governance of the club. Beyond that, I asked each of the presidents who had succeeded me (including the executive committee which served in lieu of a president in 2016–2017) to provide an overview of significant activity during his or her term.

Fortunately, in 2001, General Manager Gerald King took the minute books dating from 1881 to the Western Missouri Historical Society, where they were microfilmed. The original minute books, ledger books, correspondence files, real estate abstracts, etc., were and are increasingly fragile. So, while the minutes of board and membership meetings from 1881 until 2001 exist, surprisingly, none could be found since 2001. I believe they may exist, at least in digital form, as I suspect they were required for audit purposes.

Club records and archives other than what I have mentioned are at a minimum and not well maintained. I have been through boxes of pictures in the attic of the club and have included many of them, as well as some of those that were formerly displayed at the club and others provided to me by people. Given the age of the club and the absence from the scene of many who played important roles in the history of the club, as well as those who remember them, I thought it was important to preserve the recollections of the long-term members. Some of these were captured in a video made around the millenium and which will be posted on the website mentioned further in this introduction. At the end of this introduction, I recognize the many people who provided information as well as personal and family anecdotes. I am neither a historian nor an anthropologist. I'm not sure that I even qualify as an observer. I am just a third-generation member with a lot of fond memories.

This book is a chronicle of major events and turning points in the history of the club. I drilled down on some issues that I believed could benefit from elaboration and these, for the most part, are incorporated in sidebars to the relevant chapters. There are other topics that occurred to me but space in the book limited me as to whether I could find suitable answers. My desire to bring the book to fruition, and, frankly, whether these topics would be of interest to many others, precluded me from pursuing them.

Of particular importance are the many employees who worked at the club, some for many years. They became friends of the members and made their time at Oakwood memorable. But most special are the family memories. The club is about families — their life cycle events, memories, traditions, and accomplishments. I apologize to anyone who has some memories that they would like to share. To that end, we have a website devoted to the history of the club. **www.oakwoodcountryclubbook.com**. It is primarily designed to permit any additional recollections, observations, pictures, family stories, etc., to be posted and to be considered as important as anything in the printed book. Anyone wishing to submit anything to be included on the website, please email it to me at **oakwoodcountryclubbook@gmail.com**.

We are all aware of the purchase of Oakwood in 2020 by a group of members led by Ken Block and the magnificent improvements that have occurred since then. It would be a gross understatement to say that we are pleased and proud of it. Nonetheless, I felt a self-imposed responsibility to preserve or record what came before. You might say that this book, in its entirety, is Chapter One of the history of the club. Chapter Two started in 2020.

Special thanks go to Doug Weaver, Sarah

Meiers, and the excellent team at Mission Point Press for their guidance, encouragement, and excellent editing, design, and layout services as well as the excellent interviewing and writing help of Ruth Baum Bigus.

Finally, thanks go to my wife and life partner, Donna. She put up with my countless hours on this project, which, incidentally, gave her time to earn a Life Master designation in bridge and to become an accomplished jewelry maker. With her silent encouragement, all she ever asked me was, "Who is going to read it?"

Ward Katz

CONTRIBUTORS TO THIS BOOK

- Bert Benjamin
- Janice Yukon Benjamin
- Merilyn Krigel Berenbom
- Bert Berkley
- Suzi Yeddis Blackman
- Ken Block
- Mike Brown
- Gil Collins
- Luigi Cruz
- Andy Epstein
- Bridget Epstein
- Mike Fishman
- David Freirich
- Bill Fromm
- Ed Gessen
- Sunny Yeddis Goldberg
- Joel Goldman
- David Goodman
- Laura Wolff Greenbaum
- Lenny Hershman
- Liz Gerson Hjalmarson
- Stan House
- Jeff House
- Bill Intrater
- Lynn Goldberg Intrater
- Jenny Epstein Isenberg
- Ann Slegman Isenberg
- Judy Zarr Kahn
- Bill Koenigsdorf
- Randee Krakauer
- Ed Lapin
- Katelyn Lawson
- Lisa Lefkovitz
- Missy Wang Love
- Mike Lyon
- Linda Bloch Lyon
- Jerry Miller
- Ruthie Eisenberg Morgan
- Phyllis Nolan
- Lucy Ludwig Oxenhandler
- Lynn Epstein Poskin
- Brent Racer
- Leonard Rose
- Lois Rose
- Jeff Rosen
- Tom Ruzicka
- Howard Sachs
- Peggy Yeddis Saferstein
- Mike Schultz
- Steven Shrawder
- Mike Shteamer
- Tom Sight
- Elaine Sight
- Mike Storm
- Cynthia Wolfe Tucci
- Tom Watson
- Myron Wang
- Vera Williams
- Bob Zeldin
- Jean Grossman Zeldin

The Progress Club in 1890

The Progress Club building was designed by Frederick Gunn and Louis Curtiss in the "Chateauesque" style.

CHAPTER 1

The Early Years— 1881 to 1912

Congregation B'nai Jehudah started in 1870, just five years after the Civil War's weary end. Kansas City's population by then had grown to 32,000.

In the late 1860s and early 1870s the city streets cut through the river bluffs and cleared the rest for buildings, leaving a man-made grid of canyons that prompted the nickname "gullytown." By 1881, a year after William Rockhill Nelson published the first edition of *The Kansas City Evening Star*, the predecessor to *The Kansas City Star*, the congregation had grown and started providing religious services for about 50 Jewish families, mostly of German origin.

The children of these families needed social activities. This prompted Samuel Latz and others to form the Progress Club in 1881 to provide these activities outside the congregation's religious structure. The club rented rooms in a building at 11th Street and Main Street, and it later rented rooms at 1208 Main Street, a building owned by Bernhard Adler who was club president in 1919–1920 and was the grandfather of Ken Krakauer.

When the Progress Club was founded, Kansas City had begun to come of age. Its growth by then contrasted with the view that explorers Meriwether Lewis and William Clark and their crew beheld atop the Missouri River bluffs in 1806. Their vantage point would later become Clark's Point on Quality Hill. Lewis and Clark and their expedition arrived during the Corps of Discovery trek westward across America, commissioned by President Thomas Jefferson in 1803 to explore and map the newly acquired territory, the Louisiana Purchase. This is described in the *Encyclopedia of the Lewis and Clark Expedition* by authors Elin Woodger and Brandon Toropov.

Today, the area features the Charles B. Wheeler Downtown Airport; freight trains snaking through the West Bottoms; car and truck traffic bustling on multiple interstate highways; and the city of Kansas City, Missouri, with its reinvigorated commercial and increasingly residential downtown, serving as the northern point of the city's southward expansion.

In 1890, the Progress Club decided to build a home of its own at 1017 Washington Street. It commissioned architects Frederick Gunn and Louis Curtiss for a "Chateauesque" design. Construction was completed in 1893. The building's façade was preserved and remains visible on the building, which was in use as the YMCA's Quality Hill branch until it closed in 2018.

Kansas City's population grew to 164,000 by 1900. Reflecting its commercial strength, its $1 billion banking sector ranked in the nation's top 10. The Ohio delegation to the Democratic National Convention leased the Progress Club building for $200 to use as its headquarters for a week. A fire had destroyed Kansas City's Convention Hall about three months before the convention, but the hall was rebuilt in time to host the event, fueling confidence in the city's ability to overcome sudden hardship.

The Kansas City Star lauded the club building's design and unique status, writing that "[n]o other state has such exclusive and convenient quarters as the Progress Club will be for the Ohio delegation. … The building has all the conveniences that could be devised."

By 1910, the residential trend was changing. The club's leaders—including A.C. Wurmser, Julius Lyons, I.E. Bernheimer, Alexander Rothenberg, Henry Flarsheim, and others—sought to acquire a rural property so the Jewish community could enjoy the new, popular game called "the golf." They sold the 1017 Washington Street building in 1910 for $33,000 to the Loyal Order of the Moose. *The Kansas City Star* of October 2, 1910, reported that the Progress Club had leased the late Judge William B. Teasdale's former residence on Hunter Avenue,

The YMCA on Quality Hill circa 1960, formerly the Progress Club

KANSAS CITY HISTORY TIMELINE

The late 1800s was a time of peace, progress, and prosperity. The country would grow from 37 states to a nation of 47 states. By the early 1900s, modern conveniences like indoor plumbing and automobiles became more common. The move from rural America to the cities continued.

In Kansas City, the 1880s and 1890s echoed national trends. William Rockhill Nelson and a partner launched *The Kansas City Evening Star* in 1880, bringing a daily newspaper to town. A decade later, Nelson purchased *The Kansas City Times*, which provided twice daily coverage.

The livestock industry continued to grow with numerous buildings constructed in the area known as the stock yards. The National Hereford Cattle Show took place followed by other livestock shows; eventually these would become the American Royal. By 1890, Kansas City was the second largest meat packing center in the country.

Other construction included the Kansas City Convention Hall downtown; it burned just three months before hosting the Democratic National Convention. Civic leaders came together and raised funds to repair it in time for the convention. National leaders were impressed; as a result, the phrase "Kansas City Spirit" was born. Twenty thousand people attended formal ceremonies on 1,200 acres of forested area that would become Swope Park, named for its donor Thomas Swope.

The Kansas Legislature enacted Prohibition, beginning the "dry years" in the two-state area. Several nearby Kansas towns consolidated to form Kansas City, Kansas. The metro experienced a number of severe floods, particularly in the lower areas of the city as well as tornadoes that destroyed buildings and took lives.

In the new century, expansion southwest of the city took place. William B. Strang Jr. bought land in Johnson County and platted several subdivisions with "Overland" in their names. Strang began building an inter-urban railway—the Strang Line—to take residents to and from downtown. Flooding was also the death knell for the Union Depot; it spurred city leaders—with voter support—to build a new Union Station.

Kansas City General Hospital and the Boley building opened, the latter showcasing an innovative metal-and-glass curtain-wall design. Kansas City's first zoo opens in Swope Park.

(Excerpted from Kansas City: An American History *by Rick Montgomery and Shirl Kasper, Kansas City Star Books, 2007.)*

just west of Main Street. Wurmser was the club's president then, and I. Bachrach, Harry Benjamin, Nathan Lorie, A.S. Flarsheim, Leon Block, Sol Block, and Grant Rosenberg were directors. The club's leaders retained a town location for wintertime card-playing and other social events.

The Kansas City Council had approved a new train station in 1909 and voters concurred. That same year, the city annexed territory south to 79th Street and east to the boundary of Independence, enlarging the city to 60 square miles.

Kansas City's population had grown to more than 248,000 in 1910. Native-born whites constituted 80.4 percent of the city's population, a portion so large compared to many other American cities that some writers later called Kansas City "the most American city," which may have contributed to the obscurity of racial and ethnic minorities. The 1910 Census also counted among Kansas City's residents African Americans (9.5 percent), foreign-born (10.2 percent), Germans (2.2 percent), Russians (1.4 percent), Irish (1.3 percent), Italians (1 percent), Swedes (0.9 percent), and English (0.9 percent). Ethnic enclaves formed. Italians lived on the north side. Swedes lived on the west side. And many Russian Jews lived on the east side. They built a modest synagogue at Admiral Boulevard and Tracy Avenue and appealed to the Jewish Educational Institute for help finding jobs.

The Star of November 18, 1911, reported the Progress Club had purchased the W.A. Rule farm southeast of town on the Dodson-Grandview Rock Road for $50,000 as the site for a links golf course. The property's handsome stone house would be converted to a clubhouse, *The Star* reported. The house fit well with Kansas City's "beautiful residences and hotels" described in a book that detailed the city's affluence called *Pen and Sunlight Sketches of Greater Kansas City*, published around 1912 by the American Illustrating Co. of Kansas City.

William A. Rule was a banker, known for many years as cashier of the National Bank of Commerce. He had wide-ranging interests, including horses, and was a powerful man. Along with C.C. Christie, he had partly owned the Elm Ridge Racetrack and Golf Club at 61st Street and Flora Avenue, a venture born in 1903 but closed in 1907 because of Missouri's new anti-gambling legislation.

The Progress Club's member Henry Flarsheim had a business partner named Harry D. Seavey who belonged to the Elm Ridge Club. Flarsheim became attracted to the game of golf at Elm Ridge. He likely was one of a handful of Progress Club members who had exposure to the game.

The Kansas City Country Club had been established in 1896 at 51st Street and Wornall Road, where Loose Park sits today. The Fairmount Golf Club opened in 1899 in Fairmount Park on the east side of the city near 15th Street and Van Brunt then became the Evanston Golf Club in 1901.

This house is believed to be the W.A. Rule home, which later became the first clubhouse. Note that the stone was probably quarried stone from the property and resembles stone used for the pond and fountains at the current 18th hole and Putting Cottage.

THE FOUNDING OF THE PROGRESS CLUB

A study of the founders of Congregation B'nai Jehudah, Kansas City's oldest surviving synagogue and Jewish institution, founded in 1870, were Jews who had emigrated from lands under German cultural influence—Austria, Bohemia, Hungary, and Alsace-Lorraine—although several of the names suggest origins in eastern Europe.

According to Frank Adler's *Roots in a Moving Stream*, Kansas City had ... "entered a period of renewed prosperity. Eastern capital began to pour into the city, resulting in a real-estate boom in which some properties sold as often as seven times in a single day, each time at a higher price."

"B'nai Jehudah families shared in the general affluence. In the fall of 1881, forty of them organized the 'Progress Club,' which was to become the scene of glittering banquets and dances for Kansas City's Jewish 'society.' ... The club's membership long was synonymous with B'nai Jehudah's wealthier families."

The occupations of the founders were mostly entrepreneurial with some professionals. Also, according to Adler, of the thirty-five original members of B'nai Jehudah, thirteen were proprietors of men's clothing stores. However, a couple of the founders of the Progress Club had particularly interesting backgrounds.

For example, Nathan Lorie, the first president of B'nai Jehudah and the second president of the Progress Club, was the brother of Joseph Lorie, also a charter member of B'nai Jehudah. As young emigrants from Bohemia, the Lorie brothers set out on divergent paths and had fought on opposite sides during the Civil War. Joseph served in an Illinois regiment under Ulysses S. Grant while Nathan was a Confederate volunteer in Mississippi, and the two may have faced each other in the battle at Vicksburg. They were reunited when Nathan moved to Kansas City.

B.A. Feineman was the first to serve as president at both B'nai Jehudah and of the Progress Club. Feineman left Bavaria in 1850 at the age of 20. In

Nathan Lorie   Benjamin A. Feineman

1858, he went to St. Joseph, Missouri, and entered the wholesale liquor business. After starting a synagogue and other Jewish cultural and social welfare organizations in St. Joseph, he moved to Kansas City and opened a branch of the business there—"the most flourishing wholesale liquor operation in the city." Adler reported that he proposed marriage to Mrs. Elise Binswanger of St. Joseph, the widowed mother of three daughters who rebuffed his proposal. So, Feineman married one of Elise's daughters, 17-year-old Bettie. Their 360-guest wedding was such an important social event that the *St. Joseph Daily Gazette* of January 31, 1870, devoted three full front-page columns to report on it, terming it "the most magnificent affair that has ever occurred in St. Joseph."

Feineman, like most of the Progress Club founders, represented wealth, ambition, and leadership skills. Judge Howard F. Sachs, in his *A Century of Jewish History in Kansas City, Lecture No. 1: German Reformers, 1917–1956* (included in a compendium of essays in *Mid-America's Promise* edited by Joseph A. Schultz) wrote that the founding group of the Progress Club referred to themselves in German as *unsere Leuto*—"Our Crowd."

Two historic events in the world of Reform Jewry gave "doctrinal expression" to a process already in progress in Kansas City. The two events were known as the famous "trefa (non-kosher) banquets"—the first in Cincinnati in 1883 honoring the first four graduates of Hebrew Union College where rabbis in the Reform Jewish Movement were trained (two of whom later served at B'nai Jehudah, including Rabbi Joseph Krauskopf).*

Reportedly shrimp, crab, and lobster—forbidden foods under kosher law—were in abundance at that banquet. The second event was in 1885, when B'nai Jehudah dedicated its new temple at 11th and Oak, where Krauskopf was the presiding rabbi. As a picture of a wine-stained menu from the affair indicates, lobster salad as well as meat and milk dishes (in this case, dishes prepared in mayonnaise) were served. Two months later, the practice of eating non-kosher food, among other things, became rabbinic doctrine in the Pittsburgh Platform, which repudiated Zionism and also the authority of Jewish law. Accordingly, it can be assumed that the founders of the Progress Club were followers of Reform Judaism.

By 1881, when the Progress Club was founded by members of B'nai Jehudah, Adler said, "the drive toward integration in the general community had reached the point where the language of B'nai Jehudah's Jews was almost entirely English, their dress indistinguishable from their Gentile neighbors, their children imbued with American ways, and their abandonment of traditional Jewish observances pronounced."

Incidentally, Rabbi Krauskopf's first wife was Rose Berkowitz, whose brothers, Morris and William J. Berkowitz, followed them to Kansas City and, at a later date, founded Tension Envelope Company. William's son, E.B. Berkowitz, was the president of Oakwood for two terms several decades later. E.B. Berkowitz's son, Bert Berkley, is a member of Oakwood today and a contributor to this history.

One can argue that these events and this trend away from (or *reform* of) traditional European practices toward the customs of those around them influenced not only the founders of the Progress

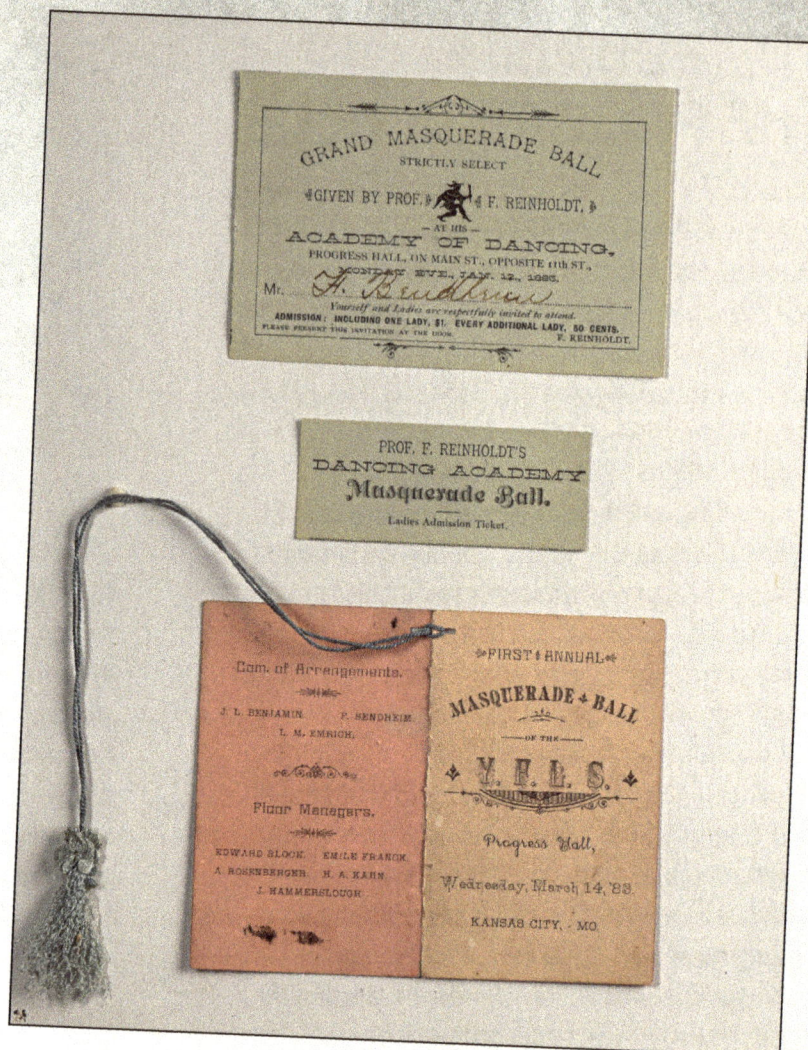

A ticket and dance card for the first annual Masquerade Ball at Progress Hall

Club but, ultimately, Oakwood Country Club, as well, for decades to come.

*One of Feineman's daughters married Rabbi Joseph Krauskopf, the rabbi of B'nai Jehudah from 1883–1887. Krauskopf was a follower of the Pittsburgh Platform and advocated the transfer of Sabbath observance to Sunday. This divided the congregation of B'nai Jehudah and Krauskopf backed down. His successor, Rabbi Henry Berkowitz, issued two sermons entitled "The National Curse—Card Playing." It can be assumed that card-playing was a principal activity of the Progress Club.

It relocated to the area between 61st Street and 65th Street and Prospect across from the entrance to Swope Park. In 1906, the first and rather crude public course at Swope Park opened.

When the Progress Club's nine-hole golf links opened on Memorial Day 1912, three other private courses and two public courses, Swope Park and Excelsior Springs, were available to golfers. The Progress Club committee was offered the former Elm Ridge property but rejected it as too costly. The Orient Realty Co., comprising a group of Kansas City Country Club members and others, bought the former Elm Ridge property northeast of what is now 63rd Street and Paseo and created the Blue Hills Country Club, which opened in late 1912.

The Progress Club engaged A.G. Spalding Co.'s course planner, Tom Bendelow, to lay out the nine holes east and south of the clubhouse. Bendelow traveled the country to assist groups in many cities, towns, and hamlets that were starting golf courses. He could plan a course in two hours by putting down stakes for tees, greens, mounds, and bunkers, and pacing off what he deemed appropriate distances for each installation. Bendelow was a former New York newspaper employee. He likely had as much impact on the game's growth as any contemporaries, despite some holding him in low esteem. After a decade, though, he gained more professionalism and respect. Locally, he laid out the Mission Hills and Excelsior Springs courses, among others in this area; in Chicago he did the first layouts of Medinah Country Club's courses.

As the Progress Club grew, so did Kansas City. The city's parks-and-boulevards campaign started in earnest in the early 1900s, and by 1913, the system was nearly complete. The boulevard system, designed by landscape architect George Kessler, stretched from Cliff Drive overlooking the Missouri River to the north, to Swope Park to the south, and West Terrace Park to the west. Wide, tree-lined boulevards, some with medians laden with fountains, plantings, and pergolas, connected most of the city's parks. In late October 1914, the city celebrated the new Union Station, designed by Chicago architect Jarvis Hunt. It was the third-largest train station in the country at the time.

Tom Bendelow, designer of Oakwood golf course

OAKWOOD FAMILY MEMORIES —
Janice and Bert Benjamin

By Bert Benjamin

I want to briefly explain my family heritage with Oakwood along with just a few of the wonderful memories that I have about my many years of being a member at OCC.

In order of priority, it is incumbent that I first mention that Janice Yukon and I were married on the patio facing the then-ninth green in June 1975. Janice and I had many fun times with our friends during our youth at Oakwood and that connection with her set the stage for our 47-and-counting years of marriage.

Oakwood Country Club has been an integral part of my family for generations. My paternal great grandfather, David Benjamin, and maternal great grandfather, Theodore Griff, were both members of the Progress Club, the predecessor to Oakwood. Each was instrumental in moving the club from midtown Kansas City to Dodson, Missouri. My grandmother, Helen Griff Lyon, was the first Women's Golf Champion of Oakwood in 1915.

I have incredibly fond childhood, teenage, and adult memories of being a part of the Oakwood family. Below are just a few of those cherished times I experienced at "the Club."

I attended Oakwood Day camp, and it was there that I met my friends for life: Jack Brozman, Bart Cohen, and Tom Sight. They remain my dearest friends today.

My father, David Benjamin II, would bring me to Oakwood most nearly every weekend in the summer

Bert Benjamin sits in the back seat of the iconic Lincoln Continental of his uncle, Alan Benjamin, in 1966 or 1967. His cousin, Ellen Benjamin, is in the front seat, and Sally Navran is on his left. The girl to his right is not identified.

to play tennis with him and his friends Ed Smith, Lester Siegel, and Bill Navran, among others. It was Ed Smith who encouraged me to enter the tennis club championship which I was fortunate enough to have won a couple of times.

During those rambunctious teenage years, I remember sliding down the snow-covered hills of now the 13th hole to near the 18th tee box. My friends (including my dear wife) were all a part of those times, including when the police showed up thinking we might have been trespassing.

During college, my aforementioned friends had begun to play golf while I was still on the tennis courts. Their enthusiasm for golf motivated me to learn to play. Herman Scharlau, our unique golf professional, was not just a golf instructor but very much a mentor for me, not only as to swing mechanics but, more importantly, etiquette and sportsmanship on and off the course.

I began to play often on Saturday afternoons and Sunday mornings, but not before having lunch in the Men's Grill with my wonderful father-in-law, Stanley Yukon. He and his brothers, Cy and Benny, were long-standing members of Oakwood as well.

With the help of "Hermie," I was able to join a Saturday game with my friends. We were the youngsters who were included in the group of Berry Bird, Don Stein, and others. Leonard Rose and Lenny Hershman were in this group as well. Even today, Leonard, Lenny, Bart, Jack, and I constitute our fivesome. It is from Oakwood's golf staff, and all the individuals who graciously allowed me to play with them, that I developed my passion for the game. Winning 11 club championships over the span of three decades is an accomplishment that I will never forget.

I would be remiss if I did not mention just a few of the many staff members who were such an important part of my life at Oakwood: Hermie and Dottie Scharlau, Hans and Doris Weyh, Charlie Lewis, and my dear friend Chef Mike Storm.

Stanley Yukon

Fred Clarkson, right, and two other professional golfers who played in a tournament at Oakwood in 1915. It was supposedly the first professional tournament in the area.

CHAPTER 2

Expanding Into the Twenties— 1913 to 1929

One theory of what led to the Progress Club's changing its name to the Oakwood Country Club is attributed to Oakwood's first golf professional, Arthur Boggs, who started the job in May 1912, having moved from Cleveland. *The Kansas City Journal* wrote that Boggs had worked for the Jewish club links of Cleveland, referring to that city's Oakwood Club. However, the actual name of the Rule estate, as evidenced by the name carved into the stone gate that was at the entry to the property was "Oakwood."

The name Oakwood was carved into stone gates to the Rule Farm that existed when it was purchased by the Progress Club. The gate has since been rebuilt with repurposed stones and plaques from the original gate and serves as the entrance to the new 4 and 5 holes. See the new gate on Page 150.

The Progress Club at Oakwood Clubhouse
Circa 1912

Oakwood became the club's common moniker over the Progress Club in 1913, with its slogan "Oakwood, Summer Home of the Progress Club." It wasn't until a board vote in 1928 that the formal name of Oakwood Golf and Country Club of Kansas City was adopted.

Oakwood's first manager was Joseph Haar. Golf professional Arthur Boggs had returned to Cleveland's Oakwood Club, and Jim "Skokie" Watson became Oakwood's golf pro. Caddies were plentiful, and fees were 15 cents for nine holes and 25 cents for 18 holes.

Watson took responsibility for the golf course, which proved to be a challenge. A rock quarry sat a few hundred yards south of the entry gate, and many rocks were concealed under Oakwood's land. The rocky terrain dulled many horse-drawn grass mowers. Watson stayed upstairs at the clubhouse most of the summer but left at October's end; J.C. Nichols had hired him to help prepare the new Mission Hills Country Club course for its 1914 opening.

Early golf pro believed to be either Arthur Boggs, Oakwood's first pro, or Jim "Skokie" Watson.

Watson helped find his successor at Oakwood, Scottish professional Fred Clarkson, who stayed for three summers and later took the head pro job at Glen Echo in St. Louis in 1917 where he worked for 50 years. Clarkson also lived in Oakwood's clubhouse and often walked to Dodson to catch the streetcar into town on weekends. Clarkson would stay with Watson near the Mission Hills club, where he met his future wife. Clarkson told his son, Charles, it wasn't too onerous a walk down the hill after Sunday night closings but returning up the hill to Oakwood Monday night was a bit of a chore. The hill's grade is mild today but was much steeper and more winding then.

line's Dodson end near 85th Street and Prospect Avenue. The car wound around a narrow road, across a rickety, wooden-planked bridge originally built for horse and buggy, and then up the hill and down a road to the club site. Many members owned chauffeur-driven limousines, and some of them burned out their motors on the hilly approach.

Members arrive for a day of fun on the Oakwood wagon from Dodson where the street car terminated.

Scottish Golf Pro, Fred Clarkson

It wasn't easy in those days to make the trip out to the club in the more rural areas of metro Kansas City. According to a history of Oakwood written by the late Ken Krakauer, a club member, he was six years old when the club opened, and he recalled frequent trips from his home at 3804 Harrison by the streetcar at 43rd Street. He had to board the streetcar, which traveled along the old Country Club track to Waldo, and wait for the streetcar that went to Dodson. Then an advance telephone call was made to the club, requesting a vehicle be sent to the car

According to Ward Katz, his father, Earl Katz, and grandfather, Isaac "Ike" Katz, lived at 34th and Harrison. Frequently on weekends, the family would drive to a farm owned by their lawyer, I.J. Ringolsky, at 75th and Wornall in Waldo. From there, they took the interurban train to Dodson, Missouri (85th and Prospect), where they were picked up by Oakwood's chauffeur-driven vehicle and driven up Grandview Road to the club to spend either the day or entire weekend.

Incidentally, as noted on Page 5, the Progress Club was founded by Jews who had emigrated from lands under German cultural influence and, as mentioned by Sunny Yeddis Goldberg on Page 63,

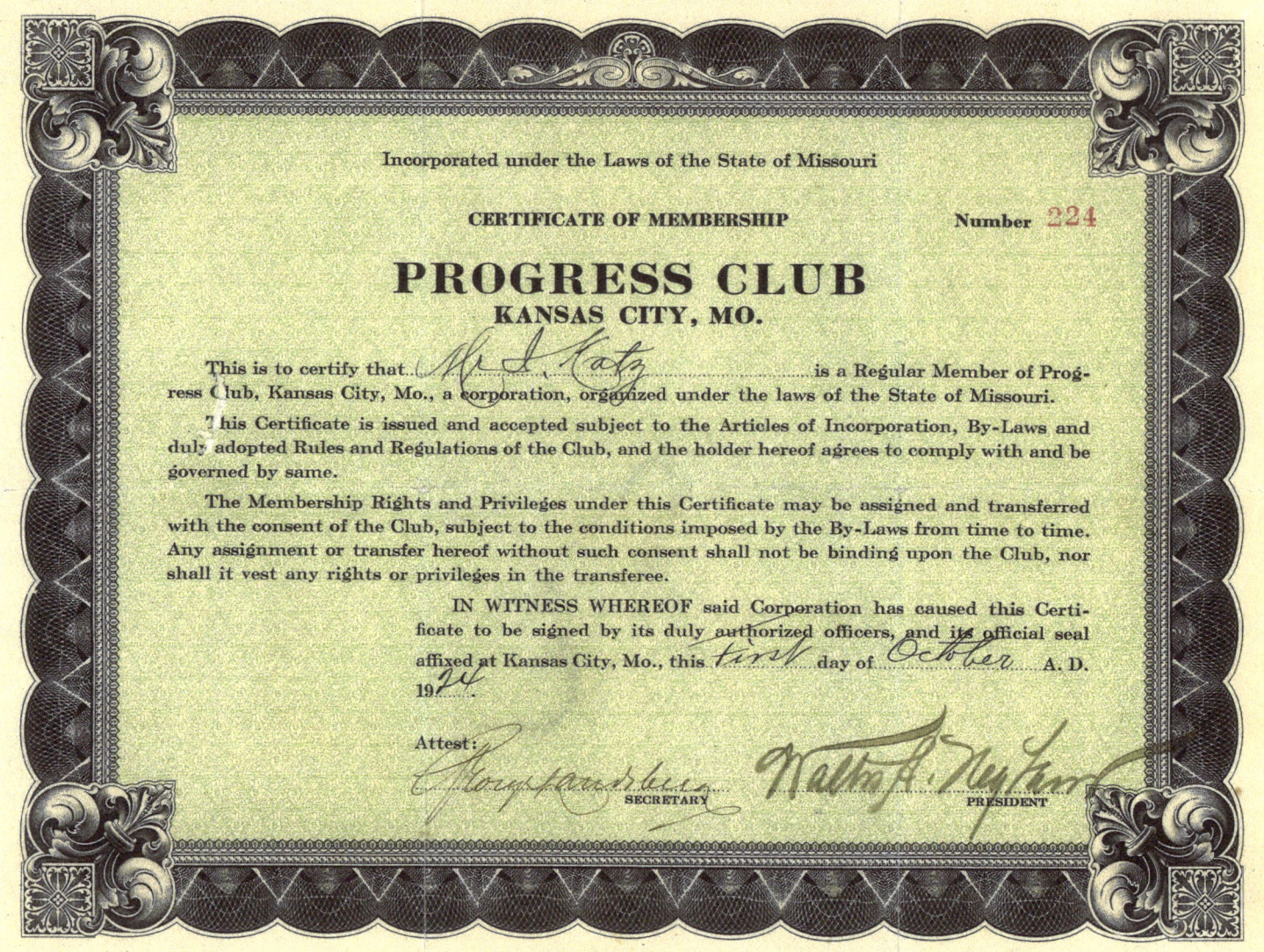

Progress Club Membership Certificate of Mr. I. Katz

the membership apparently remained primarily as such for the first seventy years or so of its existence. However, Isaac Katz, who became a member in 1923, was from an area of Eastern Europe the control of which was in a constant state of flux between Poland, Russia, and the Austro-Hungarian Empire, today located in Ukraine.

During the first years of the decade, the club was closed during the winter months because it was so difficult to traverse the landscape with its muddy, slick roadways.

One of the first professional golf tournaments in the area was held at Oakwood in 1915 and was put together by Clarkson. Seven pros were entered—Clarkson, Watson, Bob Peebles of Topeka, Tom Clark of Blue Hills, Joe Mathews of the Country Club, Jim Dalgleish of the Evanston Club, and E.R. Campbell of the Independence Country Club. Peebles won the tournament.

The Women's Golf Association of Kansas City was formed in 1915, with Oakwood as one of five original members. (Years later, for unknown reasons, Oakwood would resign from the Women's Golf Association.) Sadie Danciger, Helen Griff, Mrs. Samuel Heilbrun, and Cornelia Harzfeld competed for Oakwood. These same ladies, plus Mayme Oppenstein, Mrs. H.A. Guettel, Mrs. Meyer Shane, and Mrs. Jerome Bernheimer, played in the

KANSAS CITY HISTORY TIMELINE

The 1910s launched the age of the automobile and Kansas City joined in. Kansas City's police force dropped horse patrols for motor cars.

New landmarks included Union Station, Fairyland Amusement Park, the Ararat Shrine Temple (later home of the Lyric Opera), and Downtown Airport, dedicated by aviator Charles Lindbergh. The Liberty Memorial Association raised over $2.5 million in 10 days to build the memorial, which became the WWI Museum and Memorial. Kansas City's Jewish Community Center opened in 1914.

Entertainment venues sprung alive, including the Midland Theatre, the Plaza Theatre, the 18th & Vine Jazz District, and the Pla-Mor Ballroom. The first commercial radio station, WOQ, started its broadcasts. Muehlebach Baseball Field opened, and in 1924, the Kansas City Monarchs won the first Negro Leagues World Series.

The Federal Reserve Bank of Kansas City opened. The three-year-old Hall Brothers greeting card company introduced gift wrap. Developer J.C. Nichols started transforming farmland into subdivisions. The Nichols' Country Club Plaza soon emerged; later in the decade, the popular Christmas lights appeared.

Harry Truman and his Jewish friend Eddie Jacobson opened a haberdashery. Walt Disney launched his Laugh-O-Gram Studio in 1921 but went bankrupt two years later.

The Polytechnic Institute was established, eventually becoming Metro Community College. Rockhurst College, as well as Southwest, East, and Paseo high schools, also opened.

Kansas City's stock yards were ravaged by fire killing thousands of livestock. Over 2,300 people died during the Spanish Flu pandemic as schools and movie theaters shut down. Public gatherings of more than 20 were banned. Around 440 KC residents died during WWI with survivors returning to restart their lives.

The KKK held its national "Klonvokation" in Convention Hall in 1924. Kansas City hosted the 1928 Republican National Convention; the Ohio delegation stayed at Oakwood. Herbert Hoover won the nomination.

Kansas City was home to musician Charlie Parker, newsman Walter Cronkite, and actor Ed Asner. Actress Joan Crawford operated elevators at Harzfeld's Department store. Singer and dancer Ginger Rogers spent formative years here. Ernest Hemingway honed his writing skills as a reporter for *The Kansas City Star*.

(Excerpted from Kansas City: An American History *by Rick Montgomery and Shirl Kasper, Kansas City Star Books, 2007.)*

Missouri State Women's Championship at Mission Hills that year. Griff (later Helen Griff Lyon) was Oakwood's first women's golf champion, having won the title in 1915. Apparently, golf talent ran in the family as her grandson, Bert Benjamin, won Oakwood's Men's Golf Championship eleven times in three decades.

Other activities took place at the club during this decade. Fannie Benjamin ran a free camp for new American children in 1914 and 1915 at Oakwood. Summer cottages were located near the pool for families to enjoy. An employee house was also on the property.

"Our family had one of those cottages and in the summertime for several years we went out there and lived," said Bert Berkley, whose father was a founding member. "My dad would drive from Oakwood to 819 East 18th Street for work."

Berkley, a centenarian, would continue his connection to Oakwood throughout his life. Oakwood was the site of his marriage in 1948 to his wife, Joan, and many other occasions.

"It [Oakwood] means a great deal to me," Berkley said. "It has maintained its position. ... It has satisfied a lot of interest people had in comradeship and recreation."

In 1917, a colonnade was added on the clubhouse's east, or front, end. A new golf professional, Cliff Booth, succeeded Clarkson and efforts were made to add nine holes to the course. Booth left in midsummer to take the pro job at the newly opened Meadow Lake club, but soon entered military service and never returned to Kansas City. The club had purchased 122 acres from Rule but needed more ground to create an acceptable 18-hole layout. Several attempts were made to add nine more holes with help from Hillcrest's pro James Dalgleish, but none succeeded.

Also in 1917, *The Kansas City Journal* wrote that Booth had spent considerable time during the spring clearing rocks from several of the fairways and that the club was planning to place a watering system on the course to connect to each green because the club had trouble in 1916 during dry months.

In 1918 Oakwood hired Charles Bell as its golf pro but he enlisted in the Canadian Army in midsummer and was gone by September. Also in 1918, Mrs. Samuel Heilbrun defeated Mrs. Seymour Rice for the club championship, her second in a row.

Heilbrun won the women's club championship again in 1919. The year 1919 brought yet another golf professional to Oakwood, Louis Montressor, who had been at the Homewood Club in Chicago. He stayed for three years before moving to Chandler, Arizona, where he died in 1927 at age 29.

Helen Griff Lyon (Mrs. Bert Lyon), women's club champion, 1924

Golf pro Louis Montressor

The 1920s

There is little information indicating that men played a club championship until 1920. Abe Rosenberger won the 1921 men's club title. Sam Bren won the 1923 men's club championship and Marguerite Levy won the women's that year. The club listed five scratch players: Gordon Deichmann, Abe Rosenberger, Sam Bren, Ed Aaron, and Hyman Levi.

In 1920 the Kansas City Golf Association was organized and incorporated. Oakwood was one of the original 11 members and was represented by J.K. Davidson. A July 25, 1920, news story stated that the 18-hole course was expected to be ready by September but that was not to be. While construction had been finished, the addition was not complete. Oakwood member Marguerite Levy was a finalist in the 1921 City Women's tournament. According to the publication "Jimmie The Caddie," Levy was one of the outstanding golfers in Kansas City during the 1920s. Oakwood member Jean Pepper won five city match play titles and five consecutive Missouri women's titles.

By 1922, Oakwood had another new golf professional, Charlie Matthews, but no new nine holes. An item in the August *Kansas City Golfer* said the four new holes—10, 11, 12, and 13—were coming along nicely. The rest of the second nine would be ready soon, the publication said, but it turned out they wouldn't be completed until later in the decade.

By 1923, Oakwood employed Bill Leonard, the greenskeeper of the Kansas City Country Club, to lay out the additional nine holes—again. In October the *Kansas City Golfer* reported work had started

Golf Pro Charlie Matthews and daughter

on four of the holes and that, when playable, would be added to the five practice holes then in use to make the temporary nine holes. Helen Griff Lyon defeated Marguerite Levy for the club championship, but the big news of 1923 was the purchase of 85 additional acres adjacent to the course.

Martin Stein won the 1924 men's championship; Helen Griff Lyon won the women's title. The awards dinner was held at the Progress Club in town.

Eddie Guettel won the club championship in 1925. In September, a magazine item stated that the new nine holes were "shaping up" but weren't ready for play. Also in 1925, the monthly *Kansas City Golfer* became the *Wester* with many Kansas Citians as stockholders, including Oakwood members J.A. Harzfeld, B.L. Sulzbacher, Edward A. Aaron, Sigmund Harzfeld, H.A. Auerbach, and Sol Berkson. The magazine ceased publication in 1928.

The late 1920s were also a time of change in club managers and pros. Philip Daston became club manager in 1926, succeeding Albert Lipper. Frank Madden succeeded Charlie Matthews as golf professional in 1927. Oakwood employed O.E. Smith and Wendell Miller, a nationally recognized course construction firm, to install nine new creeping bent greens on the new nine holes at a cost of $15,000. The new course was 6,100 yards long, according to a local golf publication. Eddie Guettel went to the semifinal round of the Broadmoor Invitational at Colorado Springs before losing to N.C. Morris of Denver in 1928.

In 1928, Oakwood stood out for another reason. On May 10th, David Werby and Dr. Julius Frischer were struck by lightning while at Oakwood. Both were knocked unconscious and taken by ambulance to Research Hospital and were revived en route. Luckily, both recovered.

Several different activities were part of Oakwood during the 1920s. One pastime was horseback riding on land just north of the property. A number of club members boarded their horses in a stable north of the club's entrance. Other members could rent a ride for the day. This property and its relationship to Oakwood appears throughout its history dating back to the 1920s and is referred to for such purposes as the "north property."

According to Krakauer's history, in 1925 several members raised the idea of having polo as part of the club, including Melville Levy, Albert Schoenberg, M.L. Friedman, Arthur Guettel, and Sidney Altschuler. There was some interest in setting up polo matches, but the idea never got beyond the discussion phase.

In the late 1920s, a "sport" of a different kind became part of Oakwood when nickel, dime, and quarter slot machines—one-armed bandits—were installed where the entrance to the former grill was, today known as The Blue Room. These machines provided entertainment for members, although their legality is unknown.

Oakwood was the social place to be for Jewish families during the 1920s.

"My father-in-law was a member, and the people of the era used the club enormously," said Elaine Sight, herself a member for more than 70 years. "On Thursday nights the big dining room was full. The minute the dinner was over, the men would go down to the 'pit' and play poker and the women played cards or went home. … My mother-in-law was in at least three card games. It was like a big family in those days," Sight said.

Planning for a new clubhouse began in 1928. The old clubhouse was razed, and the architectural firm of Greenebaum, Hardy, and Schumacher designed the new one using English architectural style. The Tudor-style clubhouse was located on the east portion of the current clubhouse. Oakwood member Isador Adler served as a contractor on the club's behalf. To help pay for construction, bonds were sold through Arthur Fels.

"We were in the mortgage business and active at the time, and we agreed to loan them the money," said Cliff Trenton, Fels's son-in-law. "We would split them up into $1,000 bonds and sell them. Arthur said he would appreciate board members buying the bonds. We sold them to board members and to the general public," Trenton said.

Although the stock market would crash in October 1929, construction continued on the new Oakwood clubhouse. The bonds were retired at a ceremony in the 1950s.

Entry monument bearing a plaque commemorating Oakwood's acceptance in The National Register of Historic Places

OAKWOOD FAMILY MEMORIES —
The Berkleys

Bert Berkley
Chairman of the Board

819 East 19th Street
Kansas City, MO 64108-1781
(o) 816.471.3800
(m) 816.582.8611
bertberkley@tension.com

July 15, 2022

Ward Katz
4600 W 87th Terrace
Prairie Village, KS 66207

Dear Ward,

Allow me to start this letter about Oakwood by suggesting that I may have been a member for longer than any other living member. This year I celebrated 99 years of membership.

During the summer my boyhood was spent at Oakwood. Our family had a cabin about where the tennis courts are now. We had a second cabin next door where my grandmother, my dad's mother, spent the summer with us.

My dad, each summer for several years, would drive to work at 819 E 19th Street and return to Oakwood each evening.

One of the reasons we were dedicated to the club was because for several years, my dad, Bert Berkowitz, was Club President. He was also golf champion for several years. Possibly club records will show when he held office and when he was the club's best golfer.

Janice Meinrath, Mrs. Irving, was my mother-in-law. A picture of her in golf clothes hung in the bar area for many years. It is no longer there. I hope it has been saved.

As a teenager, I attended tea dances at Oakwood: Mother and son, father and daughter, brother and sister, Carol Berkley Hillman, danced together and competed in dance contests. I also danced with a young girl named Joan Meinrath. It meant nothing then.

The next important date in my life that included Oakwood was September 1st, 1948. Joan Meinrath and I were married there. It was a beautiful, joyful wedding. Oakwood was the perfect venue.

ENVELOPES · PACKAGING & AUTOMATION · INTERNATIONAL

Kansas City, MO · South Hackensack, NJ · Des Moines, IA · Fort Worth, TX · Temecula, CA · Marysville, KS · St. Clair, PA · Dallas, TX
Taipei, Taiwan · Shaoxing, China

In 1994, the Berkley's held a family reunion at Oakwood, during the 95th year of my mother's life. Family members came from all over the USA. My mom, Caroline Berkowitz, known as Kitty, thoroughly enjoyed welcoming so many family members to this very meaningful gathering.

At one time, I played golf but was a mediocre player at best. Joan and I played a good deal of tennis at Oakwood and thoroughly enjoyed our time there.

In thinking about the span of my life, Oakwood Country Club will always be a place of fond memories and good times.

Warmest regards,

Bert

Bert Berkley

The Coronation Ball honoring Bert Berkowitz as president of the club was held in the new clubhouse on Oct. 25, 1930. See more on Page 22.

CHAPTER 3

A Challenging Economy—1930 to 1939

With Black Friday and the crash of the stock market, the 1930s began with economic challenges from the Great Depression. Despite the ravages of hard economic times and a decline in Oakwood membership, prudent management allowed the club to remain solvent, but there were some interesting twists and turns.

Oakwood members celebrated the opening of a new Tudor-style clubhouse on June 28, 1930, with what was called a "grand party," allowing people to escape for a short time from the Great Depression. The back nine holes were added in 1934.

Oakwood Country Club Inauguration Ball Honoring Bert Berkowitz as President — October 25, 1930

One year after the stock market crash of 1929, in the first year in the newly built clubhouse (which is the main portion of the present clubhouse), Oakwood had 166 regular members and 25 introductory members, all paying dues of $12.50 per month. On April 1, 1989, Oakwood had 376 regular members and 312 in other classifications.

Front row, left to right: Gertrude Schoenberg, Paul Uhlmann, Sr., Bert Berkowitz, Lester Siegel, unidentified, Ruth Baum and Ruth Hirsch.

Second row: Al Silberberg, Helen Altschuler, Gertrude Lighton, Beth Lyon (?), Dorothy Rieger, Bin Kander, Harriett Silverman, Janice Meinrath, Frieda Siegel, Kitty Berkowitz, Eleanor Benjamin, Renna Lyon, Alma Ettlinger and Helen Mindlin.

Top row: William Silberman, Herbert Woolf, Lionel Benjamin, Irving Meinrath, Ralph Ettlinger, Emil Haas, Paul Greenwood, Robert Flarsheim, Sidney Altschuler, Leslie Lyon, Dave Lyon, unidentified, Selma Uhlmann, Homer Binswanger, Dave Mindlin, unidentified and unidentifed.

Photo courtesy of Pat Uhlmann

The club reprinted this photograph, supplied courtesy of Pat Uhlmann, in this remembrance published in 1989. The article compared membership numbers between the two periods and identified everyone in the photo.

In September of that year, The Oakwood Realty Co. was formed to purchase the north property which was reportedly to become a turkey farm if the club failed to buy it. A group of members, led by President Bert Berkowitz, bought stock in the company with the understanding that Oakwood Country Club would later buy the north property from them. In the fall of 1930, the club had dues income from 160 regular members and assorted others of under $31,000 annually. It was untimely to spend the club's resources on land.

Oakwood continued to struggle through the difficult economic years of the 1930s by tightening budgets. In 1939, the proposed budget for greens and grounds was $9,200, and projected total income was $39,000. Yet, that same year, a pool was built by member subscription for about $14,500. On the west and south sides of the clubhouse, there were several cottages used in the summer by members who had built them two or more decades earlier.

The north elevation of the clubhouse, circa 1930

The south elevation of the clubhouse, circa 1930

THE OAKWOODIAN

The Oakwoodian has been the principal mode of communication with Oakwood members since 1938. The first issue in May 1938 was a four-page edition printed on both sides. Not unlike more contemporary issues, there was news about anticipated sports activity for the season including challenge ladders for both golf and tennis, and the announcement of proposed changes to the golf course designed to make the course more walkable. (This was well before the introduction of golf carts.)

In addition to recently improved tennis courts, it was announced that badminton, table tennis, and horseshoe games would be added to the club's sports activities. Also, new membership classifications designed to attract younger members had been approved. The new classifications were Special Intermediate, ages 21–25 with dues of $5 per month ratcheting up to Regular Member, age 35 and above, with dues of $15 per month.

Gossip columns were basically about women members headlined "Ladies" and golf called "Putter Putter." The first edition contained an article about member Herbert Woolf's horse, Lawrin, which was entered in the Kentucky Derby that year. A delegation of Oakwood members traveled to Louisville to watch the race. (The June 1942 edition reported that Lawrin won the Derby.)

In 1940, *The Oakwoodian* adopted a handsome new masthead that included a photograph of the south elevation of the club. The May 1940 edition introduced new club manager William Sommers. A limerick-laced, member-focused column was entitled "Poker Face" and a gossip column called "The Oak Word" was also introduced. It reported that a new pool was completed and opened that summer. By 1942, the United States had entered WWII and the May edition was replete with references to how the war had impacted Oakwood and its members:

- The "President's Letter" encouraged members to view the club as a respite from the stresses and worries of the war.
- With the rationing of gasoline, members were encouraged to "double up" in using their cars, particularly to drive to the club. Recognizing that members might prefer to take the street car to 85th and Prospect, the president announced a policy to have the club house truck meet the streetcar on a regular schedule.
- The president also assured members that the club had plenty of golf balls and available sets of clubs, even though golf clubs would no longer be manufactured.
- There were three ads to "Buy U.S. War Bonds — Avenge Corregidor," a reference to an island in the Philippines that had been heavily bombed by the Japanese.

It is not known whether a club newsletter was published regularly between the early 1940s and 1970s. In the 1970s, under President Frank Hoffman, *Oakwood Living*, a four-page, two-color, largely pictorial newsletter was published. The July 1976 edition contained a column called "Bees 'n' Birdies," with year-to-date golf tournament winners. A September 1976 edition was dedicated to a party sponsored by Oakwood member Robert Weneck, in connection with the Republican National Convention, which was held in Kansas City in August. Guests included well-known NBC anchor men John Chancellor and David Brinkley, humorist Art Buchwald, plus many NBC executives. There were more than 700 guests in attendance including many Oakwood members. The party reputedly lasted until 6 a.m.

In 1980, as a part of the centennial celebration of the club, the format of the newsletter changed to what was intended to be a quarterly magazine entitled *Oakwood Progress*. Edited by board member and advertising executive Bill Fromm, the summer issue was a 14-page printed piece bound in a heavy bond.

The Oakwoodian had various formats over the years.

Included was the souvenir program from the May 3 centennial gala celebration, pictures from the party, and a version of "Oakwood History" written by Ken Krakauer. In the editor's letter, Fromm stated "...this publication will probably be no better and no worse than the cooperation shown by the membership at large. In other words, if you have news, please tell us." This plea may have been prescient as, from all indications, the ambitious and well-written *Oakwood Progress* magazine could not be sustained.

The years 1985 to 1992 were, indisputably, the heyday of journalism at Oakwood. President Bennett "Bud" Levy asked Krakauer to be the editor of *The Oakwoodian* and he responded in spades. During those years, *The Oakwoodian* was published quarterly. It was a handsome, professionally produced eight-page two color glossy piece. As with some of its predecessors, its masthead was a picture of the south elevation of the clubhouse. Most important, however, it was newsy, informative, well-written and edited, and included regular columns like a "President's Report," a golf-news column called "Golfiana," a "Club Manager's Report," and many pictures of club activities intermixed with historical reprints from old *Oakwoodians* and trivia questions about Oakwood.

Of particular note during this period, the front page of the summer 1989 edition included a headline "Benjamin ties course record" reporting that Bert Benjamin scored a 33-33-66 on May 6, tying the record previously set by head professional Hermie Sharlau.*

The Oakwoodian continued publication under Krakauer until at least 1992 with publication sporadic until the late 1990s. Under President Ward Katz, several editions on bond paper were produced using mastheads reflective of the season. Starting with the May 1999 edition and for at least a year thereafter, it included a member news and gossip column entitled "Schmooze Nooze" over the byline of a fictitious member, "Sylvia Finkelstein." The true identity of the author has been sealed for an indefinite period of time under an agreement with the author. To say the least, her columns were met with a variety of reactions, from delight to disgust.

See note p.128

Golf pro Bunny Torpey providing instruction to 8-year-old golf phenom Elliott Pachter in 1953.

Golf continued to be front and center for many Oakwood members. In 1932, Bunny Torpey became the golf professional, living in a small house on the northwest corner of the club property.

Torpey's salary was $50 a month, and he was happy to have a job in golf in those days. Described as quite personable, Torpey taught many young Oakwoodians the game and made a name for himself as a fine golfer. Torpey spent 25 years with Oakwood and was twice elected president of the PGA's Midwest Section. He was ranked the best professional player in the area in 1935 and 1936. Torpey did spend a few winter months on the struggling PGA tour of the early 1930s. Once, in 1934, one of his pupils, Eddie Guettel, reached the Missouri State Championship's semifinals.

During Torpey's tenure, the Missouri Women's Golf Association was revived in 1935 after a 12-year hiatus, with Oakwood one of 20 charter members.

Bunny Torpey, Golf Pro, 1932–1962

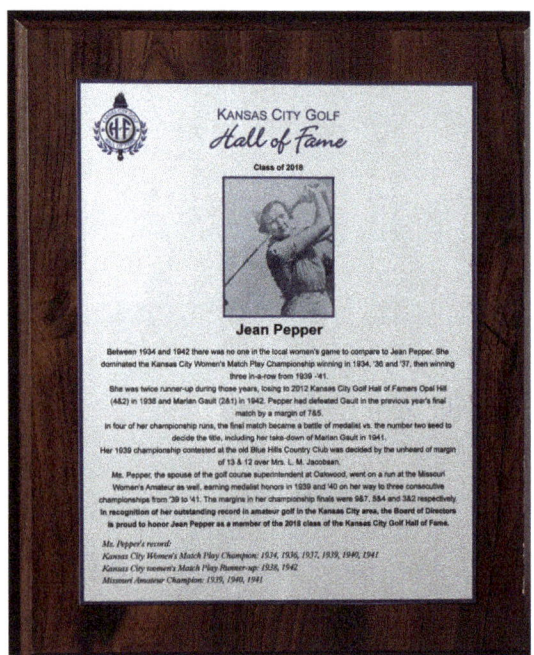

In 2018, the 1930s Oakwood golfer Jean Pepper was posthumously inducted into the Kansas City Golf Hall of Fame.

The Women's Class A Consolation Trophy awarded to Mrs. Earl Katz in 1938 (made of silver plate)

P.L. Pepper joined Oakwood in 1936 to serve as greenskeeper. His wife, Jean, was an excellent golfer and had been a city champion while playing from Swope Park. She won six women's city match play titles and three consecutive Missouri state titles. In 2018, she was posthumously inducted into the Kansas City Golf Hall of Fame. Oakwood member Mrs. Harry Terte served as sports chairperson of the Women's Golf Association of Kansas City.

Torpey found a good partner in Bob Elmer, who worked with Torpey in the shop for almost 10 years. Elmer's brother-in-law, Ollie Melenson, eventually oversaw the men's locker room. Later, Elmer's son, Jeff Elmer, would become a valuable Oakwood Golf Course superintendent in the 1990s.

Invitation to Junior Members' Dance 1938

KANSAS CITY HISTORY TIMELINE

As the United States fell into the grip of the Great Depression, and struggled with the impact of the Dust Bowl and a New Deal to recover, Kansas City found itself the center of crime and corruption. Political clubs were developed to rule the town and with them, leaders who took advantage of people at their lowest.

The most recognized of these was Tom Pendergast, whose political machine ruled the city with graft and greed. Many who dared confront Pendergast either disappeared or were killed. His powerful machine put crooked leaders in place, but there were some exceptions. Pendergast strongly supported Jackson County Presiding Judge Harry S. Truman in his victorious run for U.S. Senate. Eventually, Pendergast would succumb to the law, pleading guilty in 1939 to income tax evasion and ending up in federal prison.

Many notorious kidnappings took place during the era. In 1929, Oakwood member Michael "Mike" Katz, co-founder with his brother Isaac "Ike" Katz of the Katz Drug Company, was kidnapped while driving on Ward Parkway on his way to work. Although Katz was released upon the payment of a $100,000 ransom, the case was never solved.

Violence rang out in the streets from time to time, including the Union Station Massacre, when a bank robber and four law enforcement officers died in a shootout. Simultaneously, the city resonated with the sounds of jazz with Kansas City's own Bennie Moten and other greats who came through town. They included William Basie (not Count, at the time), Duke Ellington, and Cab Calloway. Moten died in 1935 in a Kansas City hospital after suffering a heart attack during a tonsillectomy.

Kansas City was the site of the first sit-down strike against Ford Motor Company. Despite threats from Henry Ford himself, the strike was settled, with the National Labor Relations Board ruling in Local 294's favor.

A 10-year plan was passed locally to create public works jobs for many. During the decade, more icons of Kansas City's landscape would appear including the Kansas City Power & Light Building, the 29-story City Hall, the U.S. Post Office Building, as well as the Nelson Gallery of Art and Atkins Museum. Missouri painter Thomas Hart Benton returned home to work at the Kansas City Art Institute. He finished the mural, "A Social History of the State of Missouri," in the state capitol.

The 1930s saw the end of prohibition; the sale of 3.2 percent beer was approved in Kansas—the first since laws went into place in the 1880s. Yet, prohibition had already ignited the flames of organized crime that would continue to burn for decades.

(Excerpted from Kansas City: An American History *by Rick Montgomery and Shirl Kasper, Kansas City Star Books, 2007.)*

TENNIS HAS A LONG HISTORY AT OAKWOOD

Tennis was popular among Oakwood members from at least as early as the 1930s. The May 1938 *Oakwoodian* reported that "a courts expert pronounced our courts equal to the finest courts in the city."

While there was not a tennis professional at that time, there was a tennis committee chaired by Sidney Altschuler and a tournament committee (which may have included golf) chaired by Lester Blender. David Benjamin topped the Oakwood tennis ladder in 1938 with Lester Blender second. In 1938, a third Men's City championship was held at Oakwood, won by Walter Blevins. David Benjamin was the 1939 Singles Club Champion, and Benjamin and Bill Navran were the doubles champions.

Tennis records are lacking during the 1950s and 1960s. Jake Hannas was a popular tennis pro for many years beginning in the 1960s.

Dave Kanter took over the tennis program from 1972 to 1977. Dave's brother, Sid Kanter, led the tennis crowd from 1978 to 1982, when tennis was really booming. In 1984 and 1985, Jim Munoz was the tennis

David Benjamin

pro and Mel Paul chaired the tennis committee joined by Eloise Minkoff, Leon Bloch, Kathy Stone, Wendy Nathan, Hedda Winetroub, Diana Resnick, Marcia Paul, Allen Block, Dr. Robert Freilich, Tom McGrath, and Deane Shapiro.

The 1985 season may have been one of the peak seasons for the tennis program. Men and women played interclub under the leadership of Mel Paul and Beverly Brick. Oakwood joined a league including Brookridge, Hillcrest, Leawood South, Meadowbrook, Milburn, and Quivira.

Apparently, the league changed year-to-year with Indian Hills and Blue Hills being among other clubs to play in 1986. There were 26 active participants

Ann Kander near the courts in 1968

in Ladies Day tennis and 11 youngsters playing youth interclub and 18, ages five to eight, enrolled in children's clinics.

In 1987, Rusty York became the tennis pro having come from John Gardiner's Tennis Ranch in Scottsdale. York had an active season that year with a well-attended member guest tournament. And 1988 brought yet another tennis pro, Scott Hull, from an esteemed program at the Marriott Rancho Las Palmas Club in Rancho Mirage. Hull remained through the mid-1990s.

Many players supported the tennis program over the years including Chuck Berlau, Mike Ellis, Steve Paul, Jeff House, Bruce Brown, and Jimmy Zarr (playing since they were juniors). Others who were avid tennis players included Paula Zarr, Ed Kander, Hortie Brozman, Irene Ellis, Cliff Trenton, Lester Siegel, Ed Smith, Carol Wilson, Phil Hodes, Barbara Hodes, Mel Paul, Marcia Paul, Emily House, Stan House, Babs Lowenstein, Hedda Weintroub, Barbara Weiner, Ronna Garry, Kathie Bordman, Linda Lyon, Fran Brozman, Sharon Greenwood, Fred Schoenfeld, Ann Slegman Isenberg, Carol Wilson, Joel and Sue Vile, Sandra Rozen, and Susan Kasle.

In July of 2010, Oakwood women were the TenCap Tennis Champions in the 3.0A Ladies Evening Division. Oakwood defeated top-ranked Overland Park Racquet Club in the division finals. The 2010 Summer Oakwood TenCap tennis team members included Carole Rosen, captain; Lynn Intrater, Lynne Bock, Beth Driks, Ilene Jerwick, Amy Greif, Jody House, Polly Kramer, Jen Paul, Gaye Cohen, Ellen Katz, and Evelina Swartzman. The Oakwood team was also the division champion in 2013.

Club members relax between sets in 1968

OAKWOOD FAMILY MEMORIES —
The Lyons and the Blochs

FROM MIKE LYON:

When I was very young, I remember Dad golfing at Oakwood on weekends. During the summers, Mom would frequently take my sister (now Pat Brown) and me to Oakwood to spend long days. When we were very little, she'd sit with us while we splashed in the baby pool. When we were a little older, Mom would float us in the shallow end of the big pool. I have some recollection of Mom dunking Pat to teach her to hold her breath. She'd bounce her in the water and count, "one ... two ... three!" and blow in Pat's face and then a quick dunk and laughter and praise while Pat sputtered and tried to get the water out of her eyes.

Mom taught us how to swim, to dive off the edge, float on our backs, and swim underwater. Eventually we could swim in the "deep end" and use the diving board. Pat and I both became good swimmers and divers, and we won lots of blue ribbons at Oakwood swim meets (and at other clubs' meets as well). Pat was a fish and small for her age. She was a terrific diver and strong swimmer! I loved swimming and diving and swim meets. I remember Mom would sunbathe, smoke cigarettes, and sip a cool drink on one of the poolside chaises while chatting with other young mothers. Oakwood had a snack bar and grill that was a central feature of our visits. I knew our membership number and was eventually empowered to order hamburgers and French fries and ESPECIALLY cherry phosphates!

My grandmother (Oma Beth [Lyon]) and great-grandmother (Oma Rose [Ripley]) used to play gin in the card room with the other ladies. My grandfather Poppy (Les Lyon) played in the card room, too, but only with other gentlemen. Most of the women smoked cigarettes. Poppy smoked cigarettes, a pipe, and occasionally a cigar. My father smoked cigarettes and a pipe. Mom smoked cigarettes. Almost everybody smoked back then. My parents' closest

Lee Lyon in 1940

circle of friends called themselves the "BLORBs": Bert and Joan Berkley, my mom and dad, Geoff and Ruthann Oelsner, Jimmy and Ellie Rieger, and Gene and Saurine Brown. They all smoked. Jimmy Rieger was tall and slender and always well-dressed. He was president of Mercantile Bank and he was color blind, so Ellie picked out his wardrobe every day. Jimmy was a compulsive perfectionist in everything. He insisted that I always greet him with a "Hello Jimmy" and a firm handshake while looking him straight in the eye. Ellie was a tall, olive-skinned beauty with a big voice and a big personality and was totally lovable and a bit domineering. When Ellie developed lung cancer, it literally sucked the life out of her. Her rapid decline and painful death shook my parents and the remaining BLORBs to their core and they all quit smoking. All were Oakwood members (except maybe the Oelsners?). All of them except for Bert Berkley are gone now. Bert is amazing!

Anyway, from my earliest memories through high school, Oakwood was a big part of my life—swimming, diving—and a central feature of my parents' social life—a frequent destination for parties, weddings, birthdays, and anniversaries. After Linda and I married, Dick and Annette and their (our) family often had weekend lunches and dinners at Oakwood, and the frequent Bloch family reunion lunches and dinners were usually held in the private dining rooms at Oakwood. Linda loved to golf and play tennis there (and lunch and socialize). That is all very recent history.

Lee Lyon in 2000

FROM LINDA BLOCH LYON:

My dad's (Richard Bloch's) parents, Hortense and Leon Bloch Sr., stayed on the property when they had cottages in the summer. My nuclear family didn't belong when I was young because my parents didn't think they could afford it (even though some of their friends who couldn't afford it DID belong). I don't remember how old I was when we joined, but my sisters and I went away to an eight-week camp each summer and had a pool in our backyard, so we didn't use Oakwood much. My first wedding reception was there; the foyer was covered in flowers! (We had a "palate-cleanser" course, and my grandmother thought it was dessert and left right after!)

I loved playing golf and tennis—and eating (favorites = salad bar and tuna salad)—there from the 1980s until the club changed ownership. And the camp was great for my two sons in the '80s and early '90s.

From left to right: Dick Silberman, Frank Hoffman, Clayton Barnett, and Dick Mindlin—good, young golfers in the 1940s

CHAPTER 4
The War Years—
1940 to 1949

The decade of the 1940s was a time of tumultuous change as the United States joined World War II. The country first converted to a wartime economy, with many serving in the military, women going to work, and shortages of every kind.

At the start of the decade, Oakwood put on a push to recruit new young members with a membership fee of only $100. Charles Tucker was the club's president. William Sommers was named club manager in the same year, replacing Phil Daston.

As the United States geared up to assist the Allies and eventually enter World War II, Oakwood was forced to make many adjustments, with golf taking a back seat. Equipment, especially golf balls, was in limited supply. Gasoline and food rationing took their toll. In 1942, the golf course was reduced to nine holes for the duration of the war, and when Oakwood golf professional Bunny Torpey was drafted for military service, no successor was named. The golf operation had been entrusted to a caretaker operation after 1942. The pro shop inventory was sold to the Palace Clothing Co., which was led by Oakwood members Arthur and Eddie Guettel and Bill Silberman.

In September 1942, member dues were reduced to $11 a month for the remainder of the fiscal year; by 1945, dues returned to the regular monthly level of $13.50, plus tax! With many members off to war, club leadership decided to suspend the dues of any member serving in the armed forces. It was very difficult to find sufficient help to staff the kitchen, maintenance facilities, and the golf course. For some time, members were allowed only one meat portion due to rationing with no "seconds" allowed. Tipping was only permitted for shoe shining and card services.

There was no New Year's party in 1942—a standard celebration at the club.

Minutes from one board meeting stated that business would be "conducted on the most economical possible scale." Cost-cutting continued throughout the war years. Social gatherings continued throughout the decade but in a more limited manner until the post-war years, yet holiday parties were well attended.

At one point, some members advocated for shutting the club down but were unsuccessful in the attempt to do so. According to a March 1943 letter from Oakwood President Bert Berkowitz to members, the Windemere Investment Company was interested in purchasing the club, complete with its furnishings and equipment. Although a 60-day option was provided on the sale, it never took place.

Rules and regulations and member roster, 1948

Golf Pro Bunny Torpey and Dick Silberman in the 1940s

KANSAS CITY HISTORY TIMELINE

Like the nation itself, Kansas City experienced big changes during the 1940s.

The Pendergast era came to an end. Reformers swept into Kansas City's city hall, ending the era of corruption and violence that came with it. Thomas Pendergast was paroled after serving one year in the penitentiary. Pendergast died in 1945 at Menorah Hospital; Harry Truman attended his funeral. John B. Gage became mayor and L.P. Cookingham served as city manager; both names still resonate in the city today.

In business, Kansas City factories and companies were buzzing, helping supply the war effort. So many workers came to the metro area that the Kansas City School District had to hire extra teachers to meet demand. Hallmark Cards introduced its slogan, "When You Care Enough to Send the Very Best," which would remain for decades. Kansas City's Charlie Parker, along with other musicians, created a new style known as "bebop."

In 1945, Harry Truman was sworn in as U.S. vice president; four months later he became president after the death of Franklin Roosevelt. Truman invited British Prime Minister Winston Churchill to Missouri where he delivered the "Iron Curtain" speech, and the Cold War began. In 1948, Truman ran for president and won, defying the pollsters. Truman made major decisions during his presidency: dropping the atomic bomb on Japan, recognizing the state of Israel, and desegregating the armed forces.

Post war, Kansas City annexed 250 square miles to the south. Blacks were permitted to move north of 27th Street with residential neighborhoods popping up south and east of Troost. The University of Kansas City admitted its first Black student. However, unfair housing and lending practices continued with redlining and segregation in the schools.

By the end of this decade, WDAF-TV was the first station in Kansas City to begin regular television programming, and the city experienced its first widespread polio outbreak.

(Excerpted from Kansas City: An American History *by Rick Montgomery and Shirl Kasper, Kansas City Star Books, 2007.)*

Changes to various areas of Oakwood's operations continued during the mid-1940s. According to Ken Krakauer's history of Oakwood, in the area of golf, a man with the last name of McQueen was paid $150 a month to operate the pro shop from May 1944 until sometime in 1945 when golf professional R.E. "Bumps" Barnes was brought in to run things. Former professional Torpey was discharged from the service in November 1945 and formally requested his old job at Oakwood. Complying with federal rules regarding the employment of returning veterans, Torpey returned to Oakwood and was paid $250 a month plus his meals but did not return to the house he'd lived in on the property. The house had been transferred to another Oakwood employee family, the Melensons; Ollie Melenson served as the men's locker room attendant.

Longtime employee, friend, and men's locker room attendant Charlie Lewis came to Oakwood during those years. Oakwood had many facilities on site that are now demolished. Members' horses were boarded at the Oakwood Riding Academy north of the main entrance. Summer cottages near the swimming pool and the employee residence near the parking lots west end were later removed.

Staffing changes continued throughout the 1940s. Club Manager William Sommers left in 1944 and was replaced by Paul Brantley. Greenskeeper Pepper was replaced in 1946 by L.E. Lambert.

Longtime Oakwood member Betty Barnett spent quite a bit of her youth at the club, eventually teaching swimming lessons to other members including Julie Lapin Gerson and Tommy Davidson. She recalled having her bridal dinner at the club as well. While the war years were challenging, some fun things did happen at the club, Barnett said.

Charlie Lewis, locker room attendant and bartender, was a friend to many members.

Ann Meinrath Kander at Oakwood Pool, circa 1940

Audrey Aaron at Oakwood Pool, circa 1940

"During the war, John Kander [who later wrote the musicals Cabaret, Chicago, and many others] and Audrey [Milgram] Klein and a bunch of us teenagers wrote and performed in a play called We Took To The Club," Barnett said.

"Bridge and gin games flourished among the older set, men like Herbert Woolf—whose horse, Lawrin, won the 1938 Kentucky Derby—and Arthur Guettel, who owned the Palace Clothing Company," she said. "His son Henry was my very first boyfriend. Henry married Richard Rodgers's [of Rodgers and Hammerstein fame] daughter Mary and was director of the Theatre Development Fund in New York for many years."

On October 31st, 1945, a general membership meeting was held for the first time since the war had ended. Member George K. Baum sought other members' views about the abandonment of the fifth green and whether an alternative green should be established. The vote was to keep the present one and add an alternative for those who wished to avoid climbing the hill.

Baum suggested buying additional property to eliminate other steep hills, and the idea was rejected. Some concerns remained regarding the golf course's condition and the need for a watering system and air-conditioning for the clubhouse.

By 1946, golf returned in full force with both nines in use. Notable golfers of the period included Henry and Shirley Present. Shirley won the first of four club championships in 1947, and Henry won the first of four titles in 1948.

Robert Benish of St. Louis became the club manager in 1946 after serving in the US Army. According to his son Bob (known to many as Bobby), Robert Benish got the job through connections.

"My father was recommended by Bob Sight, who he knew in the Army," Bob Benish said.

Benish and his wife, Maggie, and Bob and his sister, Debbie, lived upstairs in the clubhouse. Benish would leave Oakwood for a period of time and then return in 1953 to manage Oakwood again. Although a mere toddler at the time, Bobby has fun memories living in the Oakwood clubhouse.

He recalled going to the kitchen on many occasions to visit John Nagy, the baker. Nagy, who was from Hungary, had worked for Robert Benish during his Army days. "To a child, he was a pudgy magician in white," said Bobby Benish. "He would say, 'Hold out your hand.' When I did, he would drop a few raisins or chocolate decorettes in my palm and more in my sister's hand. He was the best chef in Kansas City and drank a fifth of whiskey a day but that never got in the way of putting up an excellent meal," said Benish. He said it was Nagy who introduced *schnecken* (German for snail), a delicious cinnamon, raisin, pecan sticky bun that looked like a snail because of its shape. "America discovered [the treat] a quarter-century later and sold giant, paler versions in shopping malls. They were at Oakwood before 1950. And I never forgot how wonderful they were," he said.

Over his years at Oakwood, Bobby Benish worked several jobs at the club—cleaning the grill, as a steward in the dining room, and returning during his college years to park cars. The memories hold a warm place in his heart.

Although the '40s was a challenging decade, Oakwood continued to play an important role in the social life of its members. It was a place to be with family and a place to be seen. Music provided fathers a chance to dance with their daughters, and mothers danced proudly with their sons. Many weddings took place including that of member Bert Berkley and his wife, Joan, in 1948.

"For me, it is a living part of history that we were married there," Berkley said.

West side of clubhouse before 1950s addition

OAKWOOD FAMILY MEMORIES —
Ann Slegman Isenberg

My father, Bob Slegman, told me that he and his parents, Saul and Hulda Slegman, used to take the train to Oakwood when he was child in the 1920s. After my father was a weatherman in Oakland, California, during World War II, he married Betty Harvey from Woodmere, New York, in 1946. Dad met my mother when she was visiting her aunt and uncle, Hortense and Leon Bloch, and cousins Henry, Richard, and Leon. At the time, she was working in the radio division of United Press in New York, and she and my father were married just a few months after they met and settled in Kansas City.

My father had a tight circle of friends, which consisted of Alfred and Johnnie Lighton, Aaron and Louise Levitt, Gene and Gerre Strauss, Pat and Helen Jane Uhlmann, and Paul and Barbara Uhlmann. They all were big partiers and very social. Throughout the years, other friends included Marilyn and Dick Goldman, Mitzi and Fred Goldman, Marilyn and Harold Melcher, Tommy and Lois Davidson, Henry and Marion Bloch, Carol and Dick Levin, Carol and Cliff Trenton, and so many others. They would celebrate each other's birthdays and anniversaries and used Oakwood as their place to entertain. (I know this because when I was cleaning out my parents' home, I found *every* invitation to every party this group had for each other.)

My father was an avid golfer. He won the Class B division in 1941, and I have his trophy in my office. His best golf buddies when he was well into his 80s were Walter Hiersteiner and Eddie Kander.

On May 18, 1985, I married Tom Isenberg, and we had our reception at Oakwood. My mom and I were the wedding planners, and a week before the wedding we went into a panic, realizing we had forgotten the monogrammed matchbooks. Bob Trapp arranged the gorgeous peony centerpieces. The band was too loud.

In 1998, I was playing golf with my father when I got my fluke hole-in-one on number 7, with a five wood. All the men and women who use a wedge on that hole thought that was pretty funny. A five wood. Really. I was ready to buy everyone drinks, but when we got to the bar, it was totally empty. Not even a bartender in sight. That would not be the case today. The first time my husband, Tom, played golf with my father, Tom got a ball stuck up in a branch of a tree on the first hole.

The Class B Championship Trophy, awarded to Robert Slegman in 1941

I used to play quite a bit of golf with my mother, Betty Slegman, and mother-in-law, Vera Isenberg. Every time, Vera would hit the ball perfectly straight but not a long way. She loved golf and would tee off with an iron. (She even had a somewhat ironic bumper sticker on her car that said, "My favorite driver is a Titleist.") My mother and I were equally terrible. (I'm still a beginner golfer and will forever be a beginner golfer.) We never kept score.

I also played quite a bit of golf with my girlfriend, Stacey Reines. We would drop our kids off at Oakwood camp and try to play as many holes as possible before we had to pick them up.

But my earliest memories of Oakwood were with Louise Pollock Gruenebaum. In fifth grade, Louise and I would sit by the pool, wearing our Boy Watcher sunglasses. (Just in case you don't remember those from the 1960s, they were thin, wrap-around sunglasses. The beauty of Boy Watchers was that no one could tell who or what you were looking at.) We would watch all the sweaty boys in their Lacoste T-shirts and plaid shorts coming off the golf course, lugging their clubs. We would stare at one particular member who was around our age, well-muscled and always insanely tan with sandy blonde hair, doing awesome flips and half gainers off the diving board. But the real focus of our gaze was a lifeguard named Tom Ruzicka. He was in high school, but we both had mad crushes on him. He was so handsome and kind to everyone, no matter what age. I remember one time trying to do a butterfly stroke in the pool, and he jumped in to save me. Not exactly my finest athletic moment.

Around the same time, I almost blinded Louise when we were on the driving range. Her ball had rolled off her tee behind me, and I swung back and hit her just millimeters below her eye. Luckily, her father was an excellent plastic surgeon.

In recent years, I have enjoyed Ladies' Day tennis on Wednesdays, tennis on Sundays, and Ten Cap with my close friends, Lynne Bock, Beth Driks, Jody House, Lynn Intrater, and Ilene Jerwick, and more recently with Amy Shapiro and Ann Spivak.

Tom and I quit Oakwood for about 15 years, but we are glad to be back. What a club it has become.

1950, 1960, and recent photos of Seders of the Gerson, Isenberg, and Starr families

The club's first golf cart was custom-made for member Earl Katz from a Cushman motor scooter with a seat for three people in front and a beach umbrella. Note the Katz Drug Company logo on the side. The club's board asked Katz to remove the logo because it was considered advertising. He removed it.

Above: left to right, Lewis Hoffman, Barton Blond, Earl Katz, and caddy.
Lower Picture Right: left to right, Earl Katz, Bunney Torpey, Lewis Hoffman and Barton Blond.

CHAPTER 5

Years of Growth— 1950 to 1959

With World War II in the past and efforts to help resettle Jewish refugees well underway, a sense of optimism and a return to normalcy took over at Oakwood. A summer day camp for members' children was started in 1950 with lunch and indoor activities held in the east-end basement of the building. The camp would continue for decades with generations of Oakwood families attending.

The passion for golf rebounded with lots of activity. Don Loeb, greens chairman, and "Red" Lambert, greenskeeper, proposed revamping the golf course and the membership approved. The project began in 1950 and was completed in 1952 at a cost of roughly $15,000. With the reopening of the back nine, the course was a total 6,418 yards and a par of 72. William Diddel, a well-known golf architect, studied the Oakwood course in August 1956, but his $5,000 fee request to make improvements was rejected.

Ed Lapin was among Oakwood's young golfers at the time and remembers the course well. Lapin didn't live far from Golf Pro Bunney Torpey in those days. "He would pick up Byron Cohen and me in his little Studebaker, take us to the club. He would give us golf lessons, "Lapin said. "We would play all day."

"The old third hole was a cliff of rock and they finally got grass to grow on it," Lapin said. "I have wonderful memories."

There were funny stories, too.

"Julius Pachter got a Jeep and used that Jeep on the golf course," Lapin said. "It was like a cow pasture back then. He built a little shed for the Jeep and kept it there with his golf clubs."

Earl Katz, an avid golfer, suffered a heart attack in 1952 and his doctors advised him against walking the golf course. With permission from the board of directors, Katz had a custom-made gas-operated golf cart built by Cushman, using a scooter with a three-passenger seat on the front and a patio-style umbrella to shade the passengers from the sun. Barton Blond had a summer job driving the cart while a caddy carried the players' bags. However, the board objected when Katz had a cat's head, the logo of the Katz Drug Company, painted on both sides of the scooter, considering it to be advertising. The cat's head was removed. A shed was built for Katz's scooter on the lower parking lot, which remained for years after the cart ceased to be used.

It wasn't too many years after these custom-made carts that the club obtained its first battery-operated golf carts, realizing that they were a potential revenue source. It was quickly realized that the carts damaged the course, leaving ruts when the ground was wet. Accordingly, the first cart paths were added to the golf course renovation project.

The first Kansas City appearance of women professionals playing in a tournament was at the Women's Heart of America Invitational Open at Oakwood in 1955. Marilynn Smith of Wichita won it in a playoff with Alice Bauer Hagge of Sarasota, Florida. Top prize was $900.

Youth involvement in golf began to expand. Elliot Pachter, a 15-year-old Oakwood player, won the city junior match play championship. Earlier in the summer of 1961, Pachter had won the city medal play tournament for juniors and had been runner-up in the men's KCGA Match Play Championship.

According to Kansas City golf historian Jack Garvin, "I had the unforgettable experience of being paired with Pachter when he won his second Missouri State High School Tournament in Springfield in 1962. In a brief driving rainstorm, Pachter birdied two out of the three holes while shooting 72-74. He also won the year before as a sophomore at the same Grandview [now Bill & Payne Stewart GC] course.

Elliott Pachter, shown here at 8 years old in 1954

"In 1963, his senior year, he finished 11th when the state high school tournament was held at Swope Park," Garvin continued. "His team, Pembroke Country Day [now Pembroke Hill], won state in '62 and '63. Elliot qualified for the US Junior Amateur in 1959 and 1963. He went off to Arizona State for golf in 1963, then came to Mizzou for some time afterwards. I have not heard of him since the '60s."

In addition, Oakwood boys won the Allen Mack Award when four of the nine individual titles went to team members. Along with Pachter, Mike and Bill Schultz and Bert Benjamin won flight championships, and Mickey Lerner, Corky Katz, and Andy Brown were runners-up.

Annual Golf Championship Tournament

Flyer announcing the celebration of Bunny Torpey's 20th anniversary

In 1952, Oakwood honored Bunny Torpey's 20th anniversary with the club by holding a special tournament day in his name and awarding him a new car. Club President Morris Shlensky called Torpey's contribution to Oakwood and to Kansas City golf "outstanding."

Following Torpey's departure in 1958, Hermie Scharlau became head professional. The Scharlau family's emergence brought a fresh feeling to the club. According to Ken Krakauer, Dottie Scharlau was like a drill sergeant and began building golf for women in a Ladies Day program. Hermie Scharlau was a great teacher with a tough, gutsy personality. In the early 1960s, the Scharlaus started a Mixed Calcutta golf event.

While golf continued to thrive, Mother Nature took its toll as dozens of American elm trees surrounding the course died from disease. A tree replacement program was started by Greens Chair Bob Mallin in the 1960s and continued until the sale of Oakwood in 2020.

KANSAS CITY HISTORY TIMELINE

The 1950s began with a centennial celebration of Kansas City's first incorporation.

After World War II, businesses began to expand in Kansas City including retail stores and chains, automobile dealers, real estate firms, banks, and stock brokers and finance firms. Legal, medical, accounting, and other professional practices prospered. Kansas City brothers and Oakwood members, Henry and Richard Bloch, who founded tax preparation firm H&R Block, expanded across the country and went public with underwriting by George K. Baum & Company. The owners, principals, and executives of many such firms had surplus income for recreation that could be spent on new homes, automobiles, and recreation such as country clubs. Oakwood grew as a result of that prosperity.

Ground was broken for Richards-Gebaur Air Force Base. The Paseo Bridge opened to connect the northeast to the southwest parts of the city. Later the Broadway Bridge opened, connecting downtown to Municipal Airport. With more cars on the road, streetcars and trolley buses disappeared by decade's end.

Entertainment and sports also expanded their footprint. Starlight Theatre presented its first regular season of entertainment. Kansas City got two additional commercial television stations—KCMO Channel 5 and KMBC Channel 9—as well as its first NPR station when KCUR 89.3 went on the air.

The move of the white middle class to the southern suburbs began in earnest with developments by J.C. Nichols and others. These bedroom communities would fuel the racial divisions of the city. Mickey Mantle played in the outfield for the Kansas City Blues of the American Association. However, by the mid-1950s, the team played its last game, as the American League approved moving the Philadelphia Athletics to Kansas City. As the new team played its first game in Municipal Stadium, the KC Monarchs of the Negro Leagues folded.

Mother Nature reared her head. The 1951 flood of the West Bottoms was the worst in the city's history with dozens of deaths and $1 billion in damage (1951 value). In 1957, the Ruskin Heights tornado traveled a 71-mile path on the south side of the city, killing 44 people and leaving hundreds homeless. A man-made tragedy occurred along Southwest Boulevard when five firefighters and a dock worker were killed in an oil tanker explosion. The incident was the catalyst for tanks to be stored underground today.

(Excerpted from Kansas City: An American History *by Rick Montgomery and Shirl Kasper, Kansas City Star Books, 2007.)*

Many Oakwood members also played tennis, including a young Myron Wang, who joined the club right out of college in 1955.

"I played tennis and went to all the parties," Wang said. "They were great parties in those days, and it was a lot of fun. Just the camaraderie. All of my friends were members."

Bernie Huhn became Oakwood tennis pro in 1950—a title he would retain until 1970.

In addition to the various sports happenings, other activities would pop up from time to time including the 1955-member art show featuring works from Dorothy Halpern, Lolly Loeb, and Alice Nast.

Among celebrities who visited Oakwood, former president Harry S. Truman could be seen on occasion playing poker with his many friends there.

After World War II, Oakwood members included many car dealers—Bud Brown, Don Stein, Harvey Laner, Jay Wolfe, Lou Fox (Newman Fox Ford), Leon Morse, Bob Sight, and Bill Sight. Some of them employed professional baseball players during the off-season and brought them and other players to play golf. Bob and Bill Sight brought Yankee starters Whitey Ford, Mickey Mantle, and Ralph Terry as guests in 1956.

Harry S. Truman, sporting his signature bowtie, plays poker at Oakwood

From left, Whitey Ford, Charlie Lewis, Ralph Terry, Mickey Mantle, Bob Sight and Bill Sight, circa 1956

In 1958, comedian and actor Jerry Lewis was in Kansas City to perform at Starlight Theatre. Dorothy "Sis" Katz, on a whim, sent a letter to Lewis at the Hotel Bellerive on Armour Boulevard where many Starlight guest performers stayed, inviting him to Sunday brunch at the Katz home and to play golf at Oakwood. To her pleasant surprise, Lewis accepted. Lewis showed up for brunch in a chauffeur-driven limousine and, after brunch, he and the Katz family proceeded to Oakwood.

After nearly buying out Bunney Torpey's golf shop, Lewis, who was a good golfer, delighted a small group of members and staff who followed along by playing a few holes during which he would hit many shots, leaving balls throughout the course for souvenirs. His antics included hitting a respectable drive by turning the head of his driver upside down and hitting it left-handed. He also hit a ball off a tee held in the teeth of his aide while lying on his back.

In club operations, Manager Robert Benish left for private business in 1951 but returned in 1953. Albert Addington and Leif Halvarsen served during the years in between.

Oakwood's physical appearance continued to transform during the decade. In 1955, the west portion of the clubhouse was added including a new lounge and dining areas with an innovative style. The addition was designed by Clarence Kivett, a member of Oakwood who was known as the father of modern design in Kansas City. Kivett was the nephew of Oakwood member Isaac Katz and had designed the iconic Katz Drug Store at 39th and Main Street. Kivett also designed Kansas City's Alameda Plaza, Congregation B'nai Jehudah's 69th and Holmes tent-like structure, Kansas City International Airport, and the Alameda Plaza Hotel. His firm, Kivett & Myers, also designed the Kansas City Royals' Kauffman and the Kansas City Chiefs' Arrowhead stadiums. It should be noted that the

Clarence Kivett, renowned Kansas City architect and designer

The west addition was designed by Clarence Kivett and built in 1955.

design of the "1950s addition," as it was frequently referred to, although adding much needed space and uses at Oakwood, was not universally appreciated and was the subject of an unsuccessful attempt to renovate later, as will be discussed in Chapter 6.

After a drought during the war years, lavish parties returned to Oakwood and were well attended. The New Year's Eve Party was always a sold-out black-tie event. Golf was often combined with these social events. Around the Fourth of July, the club held a Saturday dinner with an open bar. Pro Scharlau drew names from men and women golfers and put them into teams. Member Murray Roth conducted a "Calcutta," auctioning off each team for several hundred dollars. The game began Sunday with every hole filled. The top three teams' owners won the money. The Calcuttas became popular and served as a precedent for member-guest tournaments which started in the late 1970s.

The 1950s began an era when Oakwood would again serve as the social hub for the Jewish community—something that would continue for several decades.

"All my very closest friends were members of Oakwood," said Ed Lapin. "We would go out there for all the parties, especially when we were young and married. … We spent every New Year's Eve there for about 30 years. It was a great, safe place to gather," he said.

Program and Invitation to Oakwood Jubilee, 1959

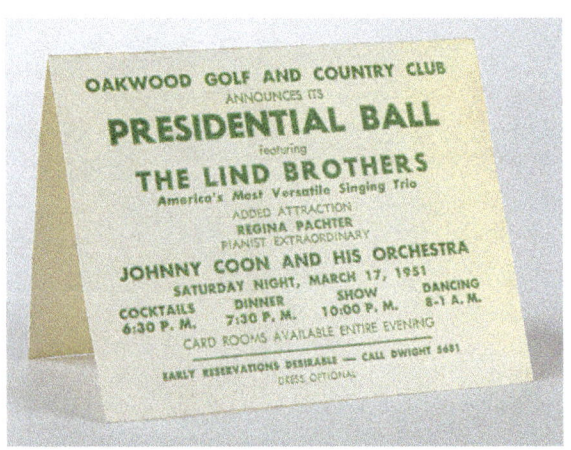

Invitation to the 1951 Presidential Ball

Allen and Gloria Block were wed on March 4, 1950, at Oakwood. Post-war weddings were common events at the club.

Oakwood Day Camp circa 1950, airplanes at the ready. From left, Jerry Pakula, Eddie Rose, Kenny Fox, Teddie Silverman, Mike Brown, and Bob Mnookin.

OAKWOOD DAY CAMP

Oakwood Day Camp started in 1950 as an activity for the children of Oakwood members to get to know each other and as a place for parents to bring their children while they were out of school on summer vacation. The camp was housed in a cabin west of the current pickleball and tennis courts where the new golf short-game facility is located. It backed up to the woods that are now part of the Jackson County Parks system while being close to all the club's amenities.

The mention of Oakwood Camp evokes fond memories.

MIKE BROWN:
I attended the camp in the summer of 1950. There were two boys' groups and two girls' groups, divided by younger and older kids. The summer was unusually rainy, so there were several field trips when outdoor activities were curtailed. Scheduled activities included swimming twice a day, crafts, games, lunch with singing of camp songs, hikes in the woods on the club property, and other things that I can no longer recall. We were picked up each morning by a bus and at the end of the camp day we went home either by the bus or being met at the club by parents. The boys' counselors were Jim and Ronnie. I remember vividly that Jim had been called up for military duty and would be sent to Korea in the fall (the war having begun while we were attending camp).

JUDY ZARR KAHN:
I remember Skipper *[sic...see below under Bruce Krigel on p.59]*, endless games of 'fruit-basket-upset' on rainy days, cookouts on Mondays because Oakwood's kitchen was closed, sometimes we 'cooked' on large coffee cans with a Bunsen burner underneath, and we got to choose between grape

and orange pop. The entire camp eating lunch in that huge room downstairs which I haven't seen since. 'Found a Peanut,' 'This is Table #1, etc.,' '99 Bottles of Beer on the Wall,' a counselor named Marty Revel, a blond counselor named Dave who we girls thought was so good-looking, the bus ride out and back (to your door!). Getting special permission to stay and swim if your parents were at the club after camp hours, staying in the pool so long we got 'pruney,' fun, innocent days when our biggest problem was who we wanted to sit next to on the bus, 'hiking' around the golf course, all our parents getting rid of us for an entire day with us none the wiser … bracelets and lanyards made of gimp, weaving hot pan holders (my mother had them in every color!), wet, naked little girls all talking at the same time while trying to get dressed after swimming, being happy …

LUCY LUDWIG OXENHANDLER:
'O a k w o o d, Oakwood camp that's the camp for me. With lots of fun and lots of cheer we'll all come back from year to year to O A K W O O D, hey!' This was our theme song. I remember walking through the club hallways through the ballroom/dining room and down some dark stairs to a freezing room with round tables that we had lunch at. Announcements were made, and we sang lots of songs led by our counselors. … Riding the bus to and from camp, taking an hour or more to get home. Coming home I was exhausted from a day of fun. We always got popsicles or ice cream before we went home. On hot days, these treats were yummy and cooled me off. Had swimming and free play time. Played hide and seek in the grassy oak tree area. Always a craft project and I think tennis for me. This is such fun remembering Oakwood Camp. As an adult, I'm thinking it was a great opportunity for us. I just took it for granted.

Oakwood Day Camp, 1950

SUNNY YEDDIS GOLDBERG:
I loved every minute of that camp. I can still remember the songs: 'Full speed ahead on the good ship funtime, if it is fun you're looking for.' Skipper *[sic…see below under Bruce Krigel on p.59]* was the best, and we had a blast. I got my first job there at 12, as an assistant counselor. We had to really work hard, but after the kids left, we swam and had a blast. Not just good times, great times. Linda Rubin (later married to golfer Tom Watson) was in my group and ran into me in New York and said, 'Sunny Yeddis—my counselor from Oakwood Camp.' I can't remember what I had for dinner, but Oakwood camp is with me forever. Peggy and Suzi felt the same way. Best of all, I had a crush on Corky Katz, and he was around!

PEGGY YEDDIS SAFERSTEIN:
Sunny said it all. I loved lunch most when we sat around singing songs. Skipper *[sic]* always wore funny hats and was so full of energy."

Oakwood Day Camp, 1951

Oakwood Day Campers on old 18th green (later 13th green and current location of the Putting Cottage). From left, Tom Lefkovitz, Paul Steinbaum, Alan Halperin, Corky Katz, Jim Greenwood, Larry Mooney, Howie Brown, and Jeff Hantover, 1953.

Oakwood Sports Camp circa 1970

ED GESSEN:

I only went to Oakwood Camp for maybe two years as we had just moved to KC from New York. What I remember most is a lot of swimming, diving off the high board, and running around the pool. We also learned tennis and some golf. I was friends with Ted Stein, Tom Lefkovitz, Jimmy Greenwood, and Alan Halperin. My mom played canasta, Mahjong, bridge, and golf while waiting for me. However, my most vivid camp memory was several years later when Ted Stein and I drove to one of the cabins late at night and proceeded to get drunk and sick on some cheap screw-top wine. I only drink the corked stuff now!

Ted Stein corroborated this story, adding that early the next morning, bleary-eyed, he ran into his dad, Don Stein, in the men's locker room getting ready for a golf game. Needless to say, Don was quite surprised to see Ted at the club so early. What neither of them then realized, Ted had left a dealership convertible in the parking lot with the top down in a rainstorm.

BRUCE KRIGEL:

In the 1960s we built 'forts.' About 25 yards from the row of cabins began the woods. The woods were relatively dense but not too dense, so each group would make forts in the woods. I don't remember whether there were treehouses, but there were tree stands that a lookout could climb and watch for other groups. We built places to sit around a campfire, although, I don't remember ever having an actual campfire; rather, it was just something to sit around and plot tactics and defensive ways of how we would protect our forts. Oakwood Camp combined arts and crafts while teaching us how to play tennis and golf, especially the rules of etiquette of each sport. My days of Oakwood camp are well remembered and appreciated.

"Skipper" Feingold would have been known mostly by reputation by those early campers who moved away years ago and apparently confused her with "Chipper" Simpson, who was the energetic and likeable first director of Oakwood Camp. Chipper's daughter, Paula, was one of the first counselors.

Oakwood Day Camp was dormant through the 1970s but resumed in 1981, when "Skipper" Feingold, who was a renowned teacher in Kansas City as well as the director of the Jewish Community Center's Barney Goodman Camp, came out of retirement to accept the position as camp director. Skipper presided from 1981 through 1986. Her tenure was apparently very successful.

Skipper was succeeded by Lois Rose Bernstein.

Hermie Scharlau leads a golf clinic for campers, 1980

LOIS BERNSTEIN:

I was delighted to be the director of Oakwood Camp for the summers of 1987–2001 except for a few years when Marlene Katz was director. For a few years there was also a sports camp for the ages of 7 to 10. Oakwood campers had the opportunity to be creative in the arts and crafts, develop physical skills through sports, and to make friends, some for a lifetime. The campers had swimming instruction from Oakwood professionals in the morning and free swimming in the afternoon. They had golf and tennis three to four times a week. The counselors encouraged the campers to be independent and to be team members when playing camp games and acting out plays and singing songs. Campers of all ages really got excited when the birds and especially the snakes came to camp. Trips away from camp provided exploration at Cave Springs, nature study at Swope Park Nature Center, and fun at the Shawnee Mission Park beach. You could hear laughter, cheering, and talking during the day and especially at lunchtime. Two special events highlighted the summer. One was the Overnight, usually held outside by a campfire with tents for the campers, roasting marshmallows for s'mores, and listening to semi-scary stories. One year it rained, and the Overnight was held inside in the men's card room. It was a big hit and much more comfortable, so from then on inside it was. However, when possible, making s'mores and hearing stories were still held around the campfire. Inside provided a

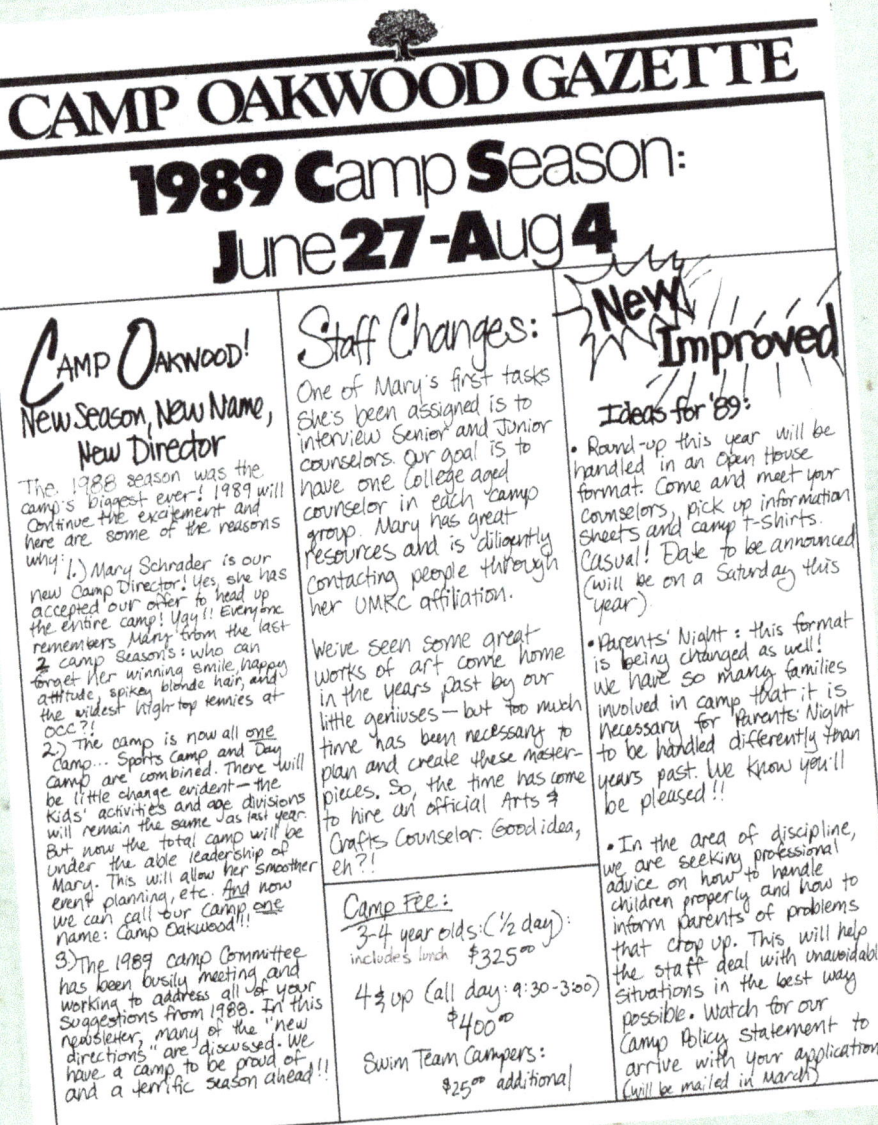

The 1989 Oakwood Camp Gazette

place to watch movies and was close to bathrooms! The other was Parent Night when each camp group entertained the others with either a song, aerobic exercise, or acted out a play. Oakwood Camp was fun, exciting, creative, and all the things a camp should be!" Katie Marshall and Debbie Minkin succeeded Lois Bernstein as camp director.

Oakwood Camp continued with options for attendance for members' children and as a place for members' grandchildren to attend on a weekly basis until 2020. However, it appears that as of the summer of 2023, Camp has been revived with good attendance and many young families to assure a good future for the great Oakwood institution.

Oakwood Day Camp, 1991

Oakwood Day Camp, 1998

OAKWOOD FAMILY MEMORIES —
Yeddis-Blackman-Saferstein-Goldberg Family

SUZI YEDDIS BLACKMAN

Our father, Abe Yeddis, joined Oakwood as soon as he was able to. He wanted a place for his family to be able to enjoy their summers and was excited to be part of this beautiful club. As his family grew, giving him three daughters, that is exactly what we were able to do. My sisters and I all grew up at Oakwood. My sisters are 14 and 12 years older than me so by the time I came around, Oakwood had changed a lot. While they were growing up attending Oakwood camp, they were able to explore the beautiful grounds on horses. I grew up knowing nothing but Oakwood and being able to swim, play tennis, hang with friends, and golf there. We three had our wedding receptions at OCC, and none of us could have imagined having our receptions anywhere else. Both of my sisters moved away but my husband, Bruce Blackman, and our family have continued to enjoy all of what OCC has to offer us. Our two children went to camp there, and Bruce and I continue to enjoy going to parties, hanging out with friends, playing golf, and having parties out at Oakwood. I have many fond memories of Oakwood. When I was a little girl, every time I entered the front door, I would pretend that I was entering my own castle. It was so beautiful, and it still is. And now with my family still being part of Oakwood, I can continue to enter that beautiful castle from my childhood.

Abe Yeddis with customers and employees at a company party in the 1950s

A birthday party at Oakwood in 1956. Back row from left: Paul Steinbaum, Donna Galamba, Corky Katz, Gail Rothschild, Jeff Hantover, Andy Hoffman, and Ruthie Eisenberg. Front row from left: Sunny Yeddis, Jimmy Greenwood, and Barbara Litman.

SUNNY YEDDIS GOLDBERG

Don't forget Dad's thrill of being one of the first Russian Jews to be asked to join the club. When we saw the club, we almost fainted. It was one of the most beautiful places we had ever seen. I worked with Skipper Feingold *[sic...see above under Bruce Krigel on p.59]* in the camp since I was 14 years old and loved it. I had Linda Watson in my group and still hear from her on occasion. Mr. Benish was the manager, and the ladies drove him crazy over the temperature in the card rooms and main dining room. There was a song, *"Turn it up, Mr. Benish, turn it up. Turn it down, Mr. Benish turn it down."* The chocolate cake is still notorious today, and it was the home of all three of our weddings. It played an enormous, beautiful part of our young lives from mother-daughter to father-daughter golf tournaments, camp, tennis, great food, to my meeting Corky Katz, whom I still adore today!

Lillian Yeddis with a customer of Abe's at a company party in the 1950s.

The wedding of Suzi Yeddis and Bruce Blackman on March 30, 1980, with members of the Wang and Silberg families, including back row, from left, Phillip Wang, Missy Wang, Bruce Blackman, Suzi Yeddis, and Myron Wang.

The 5th hole was a par 3 that was parallel to the current 2nd hole. Its tee box was behind the championship (black) tee on the current 6th hole and its green was where the gold tee is. The 6th hole was also a par 3 with a tee shot over the lake. The anomaly of back-to-back par threes existed until 1992, when the 6th hole was converted to a par 5 dogleg.

CHAPTER 6

Golf at Oakwood —The Course

Based upon the design of golf architect Tom Bendelow, plans and drawings of the original nine holes were completed in 1912. According to Ken Krakauer, the original nine holes were located "south and east of the clubhouse," which would correspond, generally, with the existing back nine. Bendelow was part of a school of noted designers of Scottish descent who designed courses during the early part of the 20th century in both Europe and North America. Other designers in this group included the team of Charles B. MacDonald and Seth Raynor, Willie Park, Jr., Dr. Alister Mackenzie, Donald Ross, A.W. Tillinghast, and Robert Trent Jones, Sr.

Bendelow was known as "The Johnny Appleseed of American Golf" and "The Dean of American Golf." He is credited with designing over 700 courses including six that have received historic designation by the National Park Service.

Tom Bendelow

He moved from New York to Chicago to become A.G. Spalding Company's director of golf course development. Some noteworthy courses Bendelow designed include Atlanta Athletic Club's East Lake Golf Club, where Bobby Jones learned the game of golf and which was the course where the 2023 FedEx Cup finals was played, and three courses for the developers of Medinah Country Club, including the famous Medinah No. 3.

In 1917, before the construction of the additional nine holes, then golf pro Cliff Booth personally worked to clear rocks to add a "watering system" to connect each green. Because Booth resigned in July 1917, it appears that he didn't enjoy that work very much. As the still relatively new game of golf became more popular and the membership of the Progress Club at Oakwood increased, there was a desire to expand the golf course to eighteen holes, but the original 122 acres were not sufficient. While several attempts to acquire more ground were unsuccessful, sometime between then and 1923, the additional property was acquired.

In 1923, Oakwood employed Bill Leonard, the groundskeeper of Kansas City Country Club, and Oakwood pro Charlie Matthews, to lay out an additional nine holes. *Kansas City Golfer* reported that work had begun on four of the holes which would be added to five existing practice holes to make an additional nine temporary holes. Meanwhile, the board authorized certain members

Gil Collins, Green Superintendent from 1965–1996, was involved in the planning and development of many significant golf course improvements.

WOMEN'S GOLF

Oakwood women have distinguished themselves both in external competition and intramurally throughout the years.

The Women's Golf Association of Kansas City was formed in 1915, with Oakwood as one of five original members. By 1938, membership included, beside Oakwood, Quivira, Milburn, Hillcrest, Indian Hills, Blue Hills, Victory Hills, St. Joseph Country Club, Mission Hills, Kansas City Country Club, Meadow Lake, and Old Mission Country Club. (Years later, Oakwood would resign from the Women's Golf Association.)

According to a history of Oakwood written by Ken Krakauer, Sadie Danciger, Helen Griff, Mrs. Samuel Heibrun, and Cornelia Harzfeld competed for Oakwood. These same women, plus Mayme Oppenstein, Mrs. H.A. Guettel, Mrs. Meyer Shane, and Mrs. Jerome Bernheimer, played in the Missouri State Women's Championship at Mission Hills that year. Helen Griff (later Helen Griff Lyon) was Oakwood's first woman golf champion, having won the title in 1915. In 1917 and 1918, Mrs. Samuel Heilbrun won the women's club championship.

Club records during this period were spotty, but Marguerite Levy won the women's championship in 1923.

According to Oakwood's bylaws reported in *The Oakwoodian* in 1940, "the course is not open to women on Saturdays, before the hours of one and four; nor on Sundays and holidays until 12:30." Restrictions on women's use of the golf course were modified from time to time but remained in effect until the mid-1990s when the board eliminated all restrictions.

During Bunny Torpey's tenure as Golf Professional, the Missouri Women's Golf Association was revived in 1935 after a 12-year hiatus, with Oakwood one of 20 charter members.

Jean Pepper won three women's city titles and three Missouri state titles as a member of Oakwood. In 2019, Pepper was posthumously inducted into the Kansas City Golf Hall of Fame.

Oakwood member Julia Terte served as sports chairperson of the Women's Golf Association of Kansas City in 1938.

Formal records of women's club champions (or, any club champions), were not maintained until 1947, when plaques were created. Interestingly, the plaque with the names of the women's club champions did not reflect the given names of the women's champions, but rather their married names, until 1960.

Also, after 1947, the women's champions are reflected on a plaque except for 1964, 1965, 1967, 1968, 1969, 1972, 1973, 1983, 1984, 1986, 1996, 1997, 1999, or 2001. The reasons for the absence of the names of champions in those years are not known. However, early records and the women's championship plaque reflect that there have been at least 15 women with multiple championships, most notably Lynn Poskin with 11 championship titles.

Lynn Poskin won 11 women's champ titles at the club.

In the mid 1980s, the women's golf program was booming with approximately 40 golfers weekly on Tuesday women's day. Into the 1990s, the women began having themed guest days and eventually moved to an annual invitational that ultimately became the "Acorn Classic."

In the mid-1990s, the Oakwood women were invited to join the Country Club District Women's Golf Association. The CCDWGA included Mission Hills, Indian Hills, Kansas City Country Club, Blue Hills, and Hallbrook. (Milburn Country Club has since joined the group). Many of our members have held the position of president, including Amy Greif, Lynn Poskin, and Camille Reid. Our players have often won the annual low-net prizes.

In 1986, Oakwood's women's golf team won first place by edging out Quivira Country Club in their first year of inter-club play. Members of the team included Flo Frischer, Diane Arnell, Beverly Brick, Laura Sechrist, Cathy Stern, Toby Weinberg, Debbie Lubin, Ellen Laner, and Pat Morse.

KCGA hosted an invitational in the 1990s and Ken Krakauer encouraged Lynn Poskin and Camille Reid to participate. When they won, Ken presented them the award at the ceremony following the two-day tournament. In the 2000s, the women of Oakwood began participating in the KC Cup, a city-wide competition featuring match play games. The six players in each competition came from a wide group of women including Kay Johnson, Lynn Poskin, Amy Greif, Camille Reid, Jill Shapiro, Phyllis Cohen, Phyllis Nolan, Barb Hodes, Eileen Cohen, and Ronna Garry. Oakwood's best finish—2nd place—was quite an achievement for a city-wide tournament with so few golfers participating.

The 2020s found a rebirth of the women's golf program with 18- and 9-hole programs in full bloom.

MEN'S GOLF

Few would disagree that Mike Shteamer is one of the best golfers in the history of Oakwood. His nine men's club championships, second only to Bert Benjamin's 11 championships, rank among other multiple champions in Oakwood golf annals: Greg Johnson (8), Arnold Garfinkel (7), Martin Stein (6), Leonard Rose and Henry Present (5 each), Berry Bird (4) and Don Loeb, Merrill Rose and Bart Cohen (3 each). Mike agreed to offer his perspective on various aspects of golf at Oakwood and particularly men's golf. As to the course that he grew up on and has played his entire life, Oakwood, in his opinion, after the Scott Miller improvements, ranked among the best Kansas City courses after Wolf Creek, Milburn, and the Kansas City Country Club.

Mike Shteamer won nine Men's Club Championships from 1977 through 2016.

Of the various improvements to the course over the years (excluding the recent ones), one that stands out in Mike's mind was moving the men's and champion tee boxes on the old second hole up the hill and cutting them into the woods. Of course, one reason it stands out dates to the 1970s. Mike played Arnold Garfinkel in a club championship match one year. Oakwood golf records do not include championship runners-up but at the end of 18 holes, Shteamer and Garfinkel were tied. On the first playoff hole (old hole number one), Shteamer missed a two-footer that would have won the match. Among his memories of the match, after approximately 50 years, was Garfinkel uttering "Oh my!!" However, on the next hole, hitting from the new tee on hole two, Arnold hit his drive out of bounds, and Shteamer went on to win the match. He estimates that, beside the 11 finals championships that he won, he played in 10 to 15 club championships that he did not win.

Some of Mike's fondest memories of golf at Oakwood were being left off at the club at 9 in the morning and playing junior golf, tennis, and swimming until 5 p.m. He recalls meeting a bus at Border Star School in Brookside for the trek to Oakwood. After that, golf mostly took a back seat to baseball until his senior year in high school when he joined lifetime friends George Barton and Ken Lawrence on the Pem-Day golf team. In his first match at Mission Hills Country Club, Shteamer shot a 36 and was the medalist. Their team, which was projected to win state and to surpass earlier Pem-Day teams that featured players like Tom Watson and Elliott Pachter, failed to qualify at districts. Mike recalls that Coach Pat White didn't say a word the entire trip back from Rock Hill Country Club in Independence.

After college and law school, Mike reignited his interest in golf. While starting his legal career at Levy & Craig, he found time early weekend mornings with brother Rick and friends David Freirich and Ken Block to hone his golf game. Annually, the foursome faced off in the Shteamer-Brozman Cup against Jack Brozman, Buddy Soloff, Bert Benjamin, and Tom Sight. The golf group expanded over the years, ultimately resulting in the weekly Friday and Saturday games to which Mike still looks forward. He doesn't attribute his success as a golfer to any particular instructor but to a lifetime of practice and competition. Besides his fellow competitors at Oakwood, he played at Oakwood with some outstanding competitors including golf professionals Dave Newquest, Payne Stewart, and Stan Utley.

After beating another much younger Oakland great, Greg Johnson, in the club championship in 2016, and losing the following year in the finals to Mason Emmott, Mike realized that the length of some of the younger golfers was tough to overcome. Since then, he is content to play with competitive old friends

Dan Scharf teeing off on old hole #3

including Ken Block, who Mike says "never gives up," while enjoying the skills and camaraderie of some of the outstanding new member-players like Curtis Yonke, Vance Wentz, Mike Snyder, and Doug Curry.

The mention of the 10 to 15 club championship finals matches that Mike Shteamer did not win brings to mind the many great matches that have occurred at Oakwood, and that could just as easily have gone a different direction. For example, David Freirich, always a good golfer and competitor, recalls the 1978 club championship. David made it to the Championship Flight semi-finals and was facing five-time champion Leonard Rose, who was heavily favored. David was playing very well, and word promptly spread to some of David's friends who rushed out to follow the match. With David up by two holes with two to go, Leonard made a par on the 17th hole. After Leonard made par on 17, David chipped in for a birdie to win the match 3-1. David went on to play Bart Cohen in the finals which Bart won, it being the first of his three club championships.

to negotiate the purchase of an additional 87 acres. However, it was not until March 1929 that the membership authorized the purchase of 87 acres plus the lake for a total of $25,000. After the lake was purchased, a road was built to the lake that is believed was essentially along the same route as the road prior to the construction of the existing ninth hole. No plans of the original nine holes built in 1911—nor of the additional nine holes built in the late 1920s—can be located. However, it is believed that the original holes generally coincide with the location of the existing back nine, and the later-built nine holes coincide with the location of the existing front nine, with the road serving as a de facto dividing line between the nines.

In 1952, Green Chairman Don Loeb and Greens Superintendent Red Lambert proposed revamping the golf course at a cost of $15,000. Again, while no plans for this work are believed to exist, the back nine was rerouted. Also, the green on hole number 4 (now no. 2) was relocated and rebuilt on the north side of the creek. Gil Collins, Greens Superintendent from 1965 to 1990, believed this was intended to avoid errant tee shots from the 16th hole. During the late 1950s, hole no. 5, which was a par 3 located on the east side of the 4th hole (now no. 2) with a green located by the lake, was relocated to its current location (now the 3rd hole), but with a tee box across the creek from the old 4th green. The tee box for hole no. 5 (now the 3rd hole) was subsequently relocated to its current location.

In 1956, well-known golf course architect William Diddel proposed to study the course with the idea of making changes for a fee of $5,000, but the proposal was rejected.

Between 1960 and 2020, a number of improvements were made to Oakwood's golf course. According to Gil Collins, the following were the major changes made or initiated during his tenure:

- 1965, Dutch Elm Disease killed the American Elm trees at Oakwood. Tree removals were started by the previous superintendent, Max Beer. Collins continued the removal of the dead trees and implemented a tree replacement program.
- Early 1960s, Bluegrass fairways were transitioned to Bermuda fairways. This did not last long because winter-kill took out most of the Bermuda.
- 1960s, the tee box on hole 2 was cut out of the woods creating a chute. This was part of the need to move the entire tee structure on 2 away from the cart path on hole 1 where errant shots from one tee sometimes landed.
- 1970s, fairways were replaced by zoysia, and a new irrigation system was installed. A new shop was built in the 1970s as well.
- 1980, the green on hole 11 was rebuilt.
- 1985, the green on hole 12 was rebuilt.

1990–91, Gil Collins recommended to the Greens and Grounds Committee changes be made:

- In 1990, large-scale renovations to the course were considered. Gil recalls that Committee Chairman Irv Rubin, father-in-law of Tom Watson, recommended that Watson be consulted as to golf course changes and that he could help market the proposed changes to the board. Committee members Irv Blond and David Goodman, among others, concurred. Watson and Collins designed the changes in holes 5–8 which culminated in moving the tee box and changes to the present location of the tees of hole 5 (now hole no. 3) so the green could be seen from the tee and leaving the possibility of moving the 4th green across the creek. Changing hole 6 from a 210 yard par three over the lake, which followed par 3 hole 5, to the present dog-leg par 5, thereby eliminating the old par 4 hole 7. Hole 7 was changed

Old hole #9 in full fall glory

to a short par-three cut out of the woods since the members wanted to vary the length of par threes on the course. Hole 8 changed to its current routing and the green was rebuilt. The dramatically changed holes were introduced to the membership in the spring of 1993 at an event at which Watson and Head Golf Professional Bill Baraban lead a large group of members through the changes while Watson hit shots to demonstrate the reasons for, and the features of, the changes. Watson also recommended golf course architect Scott Miller to create a plan for the golf course. Initial changes, largely inspired by Watson, included redesigning the greens on holes 2, 8, 10, 12, 14, and 16.

- In or about 1993, golf course architect Craig Schreiner designed new greens on 1, 3, 15, and 17. In 1993, work on 10, 15, and 16 was completed. By 1997, with help from new Greens Superintendent Jeff Elmer, the Schreiner-designed greens were opened for play and new expanded tees on the practice range became operational.

- According to Oakwood golf lore, when Tom Watson and Gil Collins were visualizing the new par 3 7th hole to be cut out of the woods west of the old 7th green (now the location of the 6th green), Watson asked Collins to stand amidst the trees and to hold up a tall pole at the location where Tom thought a shot to the green should land. Head Pro Baraban hit the shot while Watson looked on. A few seconds later a scream was heard after Gil took a painful shot to the groin area. Gil disputes the accuracy of this story.

Weneck Party at Oakwood for NBC executives and announcers during the 1976 Republican National Convention. From left, Robert Weneck, Tom Brokaw, Mrs. Weneck, David Brinkley, and John Chancellor. *See more about this event on Page 82.*

CHAPTER 7

A Steady Course Amid Unsettled Times—1960 to 1979

Although it was a tumultuous time in the United States, the era of the 1960s at Oakwood was a time of stability, steady growth, and fun times. By the 1970s, Oakwood continued as "the place to be" for Jewish people wanting a country club atmosphere for socializing, family events, recreational sports, and business networking.

Golf remained a centerpiece of recreation and socializing. With fairway improvements in mind, club members in 1960 approved a proposal from E.T. Archer Company for a watering system for the front nine and the installation of Bermuda grass on the fairways at a cost of $82,000 to be paid for by a $6 a month assessment over three years, plus cart income. Bermuda grass testing began to determine if it would provide proper coverage for the "rocky, thin topsoil acreage."

The course itself would face challenges. In 1967, construction of Interstate 435 on the south edge of the course caused severe drainage issues, resulting in the accumulation of silt in the main lake, which was the principal water storage system for the golf course. By October of that year, an automatic watering system was installed for the greens. Six years later, zoysia began to be stripped on the fairways. After a challenging 60 years, the course transformation to the velvety carpet-like greens began.

As for playing the game, Arnold Garfinkel won the first of six club championships in 1963, and member Fred Kornblum served as president of the Kansas City Golf Association. That same year, golf professional Hermie Scharlau scored a course record of 61. In 1965, Gil Collins joined the Oakwood staff as golf course superintendent and

Arnold Garfinkel accepts a trophy for one of his seven club championships from Golf Chairman Harvey "Bud" Laner.

stayed until his 1996 retirement. In 1967, Leonard Rose won the first of four championships.

"Oakwood had the best greens of any golf course in Kansas City," said Bill Fromm. Fellow golfer Myron Wang expressed similar thoughts.

"Everyone outside of Oakwood loved to play Oakwood because it was a challenging course," Wang said.

There were lots of kids who spent their summers at Oakwood learning to play golf, enjoying swimming, and playing tennis, including siblings Andy Epstein, Jenny Isenberg, and Lynn Poskin.

"A perfect day for me was getting to Oakwood by 8:30 a.m. and jumping in the pool, then playing a few sets of tennis, getting something to eat, then playing golf, then tennis, and back in the pool before we got picked up by 5:30 p.m.," Epstein said. "You played and played and played until you passed out and did it all over again. … It was our home away from home."

Epstein loved spending summers at Oakwood.

"I remember at the end of May putting on my Oakwood team swimsuit and I didn't take it off until August. If you played golf, you put your golf clothes over it. Every little boy at Oakwood wore their swim trunks all summer," Epstein said.

"It was my happy place," said his sister Lynn Poskin.

"Our family did not go away to summer camp. Oakwood *was* our summer camp," said her sister Jenny Isenberg. "I had the biggest crush on one of the lifeguards that lasted through high school."

"Oakwood is where I first fell in love at the tender age of 10 or 12 with the Ross girls," said Epstein, referring to swim coach Bill Ross's two daughters. "They were just beautiful."

KANSAS CITY HISTORY TIMELINE

In Kansas City, the 1960s and 1970s marked a time of changes driven by national racial strife and its own racist past. Yet it was a time of expansion. Civic pride grew with the arrival of two new stadiums, a new airport, and the opening of Crown Center and Corporate Woods.

Civil rights took hold with various protests and government actions during the two decades. In 1964, Kansas City voters approved a public accommodations ordinance requiring taverns, swimming pools, and amusement parks to admit minorities. When Martin Luther King Jr. was murdered, the city faced several nights of looting, fires, and a curfew. In protest of the Vietnam War, student unrest broke out at the University of Kansas and its student union burned.

Kansas City would elect several mayors, from Ilus Davis to Dr. Charles Wheeler to Richard Berkley. Mayor Berkley was the first Jewish mayor and an Oakwood member. In 1972, President Harry S. Truman died and was buried at the presidential library in Independence.

The skyline continued to change with the opening of major buildings including the Commerce Tower, a new Federal Office Building, Kansas City International Airport, and the Hallmark Crown Center complex. Arrowhead and Royals stadiums opened, just one year apart, on the east side of town.

Yet there was destruction, too. A 1977 flood on Rosh Hashanah heavily damaged the Country Club Plaza and Blue River Industrial District and left 25 people dead. The Coates House fire killed 20. The roof of the landmark Kemper Arena collapsed; luckily it was unoccupied at the time.

The Republican National Convention took place in Kansas City, drawing thousands to attend as well as cover the political event.

Kansas City's footprint as a sports town was solidified with several moves. The Kansas City Chiefs played its first season in 1964; later the team participated in the first and fourth Super Bowls, winning the latter. Charles O. Finley bought the Kansas City Athletics and moved them to Oakland. Kansas City got a new baseball franchise, owned by Marion Laboratories founder Ewing Kauffman, and began play in 1969 at Municipal Stadium downtown. Later both teams moved to the double-stadium Truman Sports Complex. The Cincinnati Royals NBA team relocated as the Kansas City Kings and played in Kansas City for 13 years.

The arts thrived, too. The Beatles played a half-hour concert at Municipal Stadium. The Nelson Art Gallery was one of only seven locations worldwide to host a Chinese archaeological exhibit, drawing a quarter million people to see it during its seven-week stay. Using a gold-colored fabric, artist Christo wrapped the sidewalks of Loose Park, drawing national attention.

(Excerpted from Kansas City: An American History *by Rick Montgomery and Shirl Kasper, Kansas City Star Books, 2007.)*

However, there were rules imposed by the Epsteins' parents.

"If you took a lesson you had to play X number of times before you ever got to take another lesson," Poskin said.

"Our dad allowed us to have three things a day from the grill but not soda pop or candy bars," Poskin said. "The receipts were on a ticket stand and we would take out tickets and put them in piles and see which one of us spent the least."

"You got in trouble if you went over your ticket limit," said sister Jenny Isenberg.

Poskin would go on to become a competitive golfer on the local circuit, winning numerous awards. She was also part of Oakwood's team that won the Kansas City Golf Association's Ladies Championship in 1998. She also met her husband, Joe, at Oakwood. Joe was a caddy at Oakwood who went on to earn an Evans Scholarship at the University of Missouri, Columbia, a program happily supported by Oakwood. They raised their kids at the club, and Lynn became very active, overseeing Oakwood's swim team. She was instrumental in getting the swim team into the competitive country club swim league, "and that was a big deal," she said.

Michael Schultz fondly recalled spending summers at Oakwood. "The camp was where the tennis courts are now," Schultz said. "It was a fun four weeks. We went into the woods and down to the lake. It was a fully Jewish camp but with no religious overtones. It was a center of life for a lot of us for a number of years. It was a fun, bonding experience."

In the aquatics area, Bill Ross came to Oakwood in the summer of 1978 to serve as pool manager and coordinator of sports activities. Ultimately, Ross would spend 23 summers at Oakwood, helping kids develop their skills. He would also be part of the effort to bring a new pool to Oakwood in the 1980s. Ross spent the winters teaching and coaching at Paseo and later Westport high schools as well as the University of Missouri-Kansas City. Retiring in 2001, Ross was nominated to the Missouri Sports Hall of Fame in 2006.

Bill Ross

Tommy Davidson enjoying the pool in 1968

From left, Elliott Pachter, DeeDee Sharlip, Mary Loeb, unknown, Arlene Kanter, Carol Brickman, Leslie Jo Katz

OAKWOOD SWIM TEAM

Well before Oakwood had an organized swim team, there was an ad hoc group of swimmers and divers at Oakwood Day Camp in the early 1950s who you could say were the swim and dive team of its time

In the 1960s, Oakwood launched a swim team that competed in a league including Hillcrest Country Club, Redgate Swim Club, Crackernack Country Club, and Blue Springs Country Club.

The swimmers, including children of the Block, Bird, Davidson, Wolfe, Greenbaum, Epstein, Maizlish, Lyon, Fox, and Galamba families, competed in backstroke, breaststroke, butterfly, freestyle, medley and freestyle relays, and diving. After meets, the team families met at either Zeppi's Pizza or the Dairy Queen at 95th and Holmes. This program continued through the early 1980s when the league disbanded.

About eight years later, Oakwood's pool manager, Coach Bill Ross, arranged for interested kids to participate in the "B" meets in the Country Club Swim Association of Kansas City (CCSAKC), held a day prior to the "A" swim and dive meets. When the league decided to hold A and B swim meets on one day and diving on another, Bill suggested that Oakwood apply to join. By this time, many of those

A 1990s swim and dive team

who swam in the previous league while growing up had children of their own and were eager to participate.

Since being in the CCSAKC required specific pool dimensions and a six-lane pool (Oakwood had a four-lane pool at the time), Bruce Krigel, Lynn Poskin, and Jenny Isenberg proposed a pool renovation to the board. Under the leadership of Oakwood president Stan House, the project was approved, and in 1990, Oakwood was accepted as a full league member joining Kansas City Country Club, Mission Hills

Country Club, Carriage Club, Indian Hills Country Club, Blue Hills Country Club, Leawood South Country Club, Brookridge Country Club, Milburn Country Club, and Hallbrook Country Club.

Team Oakwood was much smaller than any of the other clubs and routinely came in last place. Team members sometimes swam in heats above their age levels to fill gaps in the older age groups. But the team thoroughly enjoyed the league and friendly competition against kids in their own neighborhoods and schools.

Hosting end-of-year championships rotated among the 10 clubs. A club would first host a two-day A and B dive championship and then the following year, swim championships. They would welcome thousands of swimmers and their families over the course of three days.

By the time Oakwood hosted its first swim championship, chaired by Lynne Bock and Lynn Poskin, the team was coached by Barb Kueffer. Cindy Tucci was the chair of the Swim and Dive Committee. That year, Oakwood came in sixth overall and had around 70 swimmers and divers.

In addition to the families of former swimmers and divers, many other children joined in the fun including the Bortnicks, Bocks, Ellises, Taubers, Blackmans, Tuccis, Kramers, Kims, Slosburgs, Hamptons, and Grossmans.

Several Oakwoodians have won special awards through the Country Club Swim Association of Kansas City. Hannah Bortnick won the Wally Daniels Award in 2012 and Tommy Poskin won it in 2015. This award is given to a graduating senior swimmer or diver who demonstrates team spirit, sportsmanship toward team members and opponents, and a willingness to work with younger swimmers. Lynne Bock won the Outstanding Volunteer award in 2006 and Lynn and Joe Poskin won it in 2014.

Oakwood Swim and Dive team was a very memorable part of the Oakwood family experience.

From left, Bobby (blue shirt) Sight, Sydney House, and Tommy Poskin at a swim meet in the early 2000s

Wally Daniels Award for Sportsmanship awarded to Tommy Poskin, 2015

The Oakwood Swim and Dive Team, 2002

The Oakwood Swim and Dive Team, 2009

The Oakwood Swim and Dive team, 2012

Social Side of Life

In the early 1960s, there were few country clubs in Kansas City that Jews could belong to, which played a part in Oakwood's ongoing success. Oakwood continued to build on its reputation of having "great parties and the best food in Kansas City of any club," according to Bill Fromm.

Elaine Sight recalled the 1960s as a vibrant time in the club's life.

"It was very, very crowded and a very big part of people's lives and people of all age groups," Sight said. "It was like a big family in those days."

On Saturday nights, the bar was packed. "There was always action," Sight said.

Barbie and Allan Lefko in the mid-1960s

The club was also a popular wedding location.

"Everyone I knew in KC had their wedding at Oakwood and they kept getting more spectacular," Sight said. "Bob Trapp would do weddings, putting fabrics on the wall and get big-name bands to come out. Four to five couples would get together and host black-tie parties. You had so many people you would give the party for two nights."

When not absorbed with his business, Alaskan Fur Company, Myron Wang could be found at Oakwood. Wang joined Oakwood when he graduated from college and used the club for both business and pleasure, including his wedding to his wife, Nikki. Later, Wang's two children would also get married at Oakwood.

"It was a good place to connect," Wang said. "The roster of Oakwood was the roster of Alaskan Fur Company. For the women's lunch at Christmas, we would do a fashion show over the years. A lot of members selected items and wore them home."

Wang said the tradition of the holiday fur fashion show continued for years. An avid golfer, Wang would play every Saturday and Sunday with a group of eight.

"We would usually have lunch, play golf, and meet our wives for dinner," he said. "Oakwood always had a chicken dinner on Sunday nights."

There was plenty of fun for the kids, too.

"Fourth of July was a special day because it would bring everybody out," Wang said. "They would wax up a watermelon and toss it in the pool and whoever caught it would have bragging rights," he said.

Both Wang and Sight, who are still club members, said that Oakwood had great significance as a social institution for Jewish people of Kansas City for more than a half century.

"It was the social tool for Jewish folks," Sight said. "And while we couldn't go anywhere else because they would not have us, being a member of Oakwood would be like a coat of arms."

Bus Manko, Sylvia Manko, and David Goodman in the mid-1960s

"Oakwood has been very special to me," said Wang. "In the Jewish community, it played a big part … there were Federation dinners there and other charitable dinners, golf tournaments … the FBI Citizens Academy Tournament was one of the early outside tournaments allowed at Oakwood."

Operationally, Oakwood went through some changes. As 1969 ended, Robert Benish left Oakwood again to enter private business. Steven Pigg replaced him temporarily as club manager.

Hans Weyh began an illustrious 22-year stint as club manager in November 1970, succeeding temporary club manager Danny Villegas.

"It was unusual to have a German general manager of a Jewish country club who wasn't Jewish," Bill Fromm said. "[I remember] he had a very thick German accent. He was well respected."

Greens Committee chairman Bob Mallin announced that an unnamed member had contributed a group of trees that year. It turned out that Mallin was the "unnamed member."

Big Events

Throughout the 1960s and 1970s, Oakwood hosted some big names and big parties. Entertainer Joey Bishop landed a two-hour gig at Oakwood Country Club in front of a huge audience. Singer Marilyn Maye also performed at Oakwood in 1978 to the delight of members.

Perhaps the biggest "shindig" of all happened during the US Bicentennial year.

In August 1976, the Republican National Convention was held in Kansas City, and Oakwood hosted its biggest party to date.

Following the convention's close, Robert Weneck hosted a party at Oakwood for NBC in the wee hours of the morning and attending was a Who's Who in broadcasting and politics. Weneck's team at American Rental put up numerous tents and Manager Weyh arranged a sumptuous feast for the prestigious guests.

"We had a party that NBC paid for, and they brought all their personalities out there," according to Ed Lapin. "Money was no object. They came out in busloads, and it was around the pool with all kinds of security. … They invited the board to attend, and I went."

Oakwood Living, the club's newsletter, devoted four pages of coverage of the big event with reporter Gloria Hoffman recalling every detail.

According to Hoffman's report, because Missouri liquor laws at the time prohibited alcoholic beverages from being inside the club after 1:30 a.m., a special "Beer Garden" tent was set up so guests could enjoy a cold one. Chairs were red and blue—NBC's colors at the time—and a large, marbleized dance floor was set up for folks to step out to the tunes of Skip DeVol, a banjo player who was flown in from the Sands Hotel in Las Vegas.

Numerous VIPs attended the Oakwood party including NBC broadcasters John Chancellor, David Brinkley, Tom Brokaw, Art Buchwald, as well as NBC President Herb Schlosser.

Weyh prepared an extravagant menu that included everything from baron-of-beef to po'boy sandwiches with all the trimmings; guests filling their plates about 3:30 a.m. Weyh even promised to whip up breakfast for those who were still around at 6 a.m.

"It lasted all night long," Lapin said. "It was really cool."

Big Plans

By the late 1970s, Jews were able to join a few other country clubs, including Meadowbrook Country Club at West 91st Street and Nall Avenue in Prairie Village. Oakwood started to feel the pinch and some members voiced concern about losing members.

The issue would hang over the club for years to come.

In 1970, Don Stein was elected president of the club. Stein was considered a strong and innovative leader. At the beginning of his tenure, what was considered to be Phase I of a large renovation of the club was completed at a cost of $175,000. It included remodeling the main dining room including the installation of wood paneling and new light sconces and redecorating the adjoining Gold and Blue rooms. Stein appointed a Remodeling Committee (the name was interchangeable with the Facilities Committee and the Building Committee) to look into remodeling the "1950s addition." Under the chairmanship of Jules Goldman, the plans gradually got more ambitious to include the locker rooms, relocation of the pro shop from the upper level to the lower level, a new swimming pool, and an addition of 20,000 square feet (the purpose of which is not clear from the records). Meanwhile, the original budget of $250,000 suffered *budget creep.*

MEMBER GUEST TOURNAMENTS

The first men's member-guest tournament was held June 23–24, 1977, and was known as The Up 'N Down Classic. The chairman was Harvey "Bud" Laner, and there were 36 "sign-ups."

According to Lenny Hershman, in the early years, because there weren't enough players, members could bring multiple guests. So, the number of members and the total number of players are not known. Bill Sight chaired the 1979 Up 'N Down Classic. Some years later, the name was changed to The Knickerbocker.

Up 'N Down Classic Trophy

Invitations to early member-guest tournaments

From left, Michael Klein, unknown guest, Frank Hoffman, Leonard Rose, and Bill Sight

From left, Mike Shteamer, Steve Block and guests at an early Member-Guest Tournament

The two-day event, preceded by a practice round on Thursday, has grown gradually in prestige, size, events, prizes, and cost. The 1980 Member-Guest Tournament, chaired by Harold Tivol, was enhanced to be a part of Oakwood's Centennial celebration. Over $10,000 in gifts and prizes were given away, including a four-day, all-expense paid trip to Pebble Beach. Hershman chaired or was involved in planning several of the member-guest tournaments. He was in the travel business and was able to get airlines and hotels to donate exotic trips and, in some years, flights to anywhere American Airlines flew.

For many years, one of the highlights of The Knickerbocker was the "Helicopter Drop" at the Saturday evening awards banquet. A helicopter flew over the driving range and dropped golf balls. Players bought "chances." If a participant's number appeared on a ball closest to a flag where the balls were dropped, he won a free trip for two anywhere, provided by an airline that serviced Kansas City.

Another tradition has been the lobster dinner at the Saturday night awards banquet. In the early years, the awards banquet was a black-tie affair, which ultimately was eliminated because of the heat.

Over the years, the format has evolved to a flighted event with five nine-hole matches and the highly touted Derby on Friday afternoon. Participants in the Derby are the winners of putting and chipping contests, winners of a practice round, and other competitions such as the closest shot to the hole from 150 yards out on the ninth hole. Players can purchase additional chances to qualify for the Derby, resulting in a substantial pot for the winners. The flight winners have a playoff on Saturday following

Jim Jacobs and Billy Schifman at a Member-Guest Tournament in the 1970s

the last matches. Parimutuel betting as well as an auction of the teams the night before the first match resulted in significant cash prizes for the winners. Frequently, bidders form syndicates to bid on multiple teams with the actual players having the chance to purchase a share of their team.

The Acorn Classic, the women's member-guest tournament, is believed to have been first discussed in 1998 at a meeting held at a nail salon, attended by Michele Kaplan, Gail Himmelstein, and Lisa Lefkovitz. All three women wanted a women's member-guest tournament at Oakwood. By borrowing ideas from other clubs, the event has also evolved into a highly desirable event focused on fun and camaraderie. The first Acorn Classic was held in 1999 with twenty-four teams.

When the Acorn started, committee members made their own halfway house treats and had the enthusiastic support of male members (usually husbands contributing as hole sponsors). A cocktail party the night before kicked off a two-day event, followed by a continental breakfast, awards luncheon, extra contests, prizes, and more. The first and second Acorn Classics were held in mid-August but, thereafter, the Acorn was scheduled in late July until it was moved to June, when it now occurs.

The Acorn Classic, like the Knickerbocker, has become a highly desirable event for golfers throughout Kansas City.

From left, Jill Shapiro, Kathy Shapiro, Carol Freirich, and Sharon Spiegelglass at an Acorn Classic

From left, unknown, Ruthie Eisenberg Morgan, Jane Jarman, Mary Lemke, J.R. Rotarius, Phyllis Nolan, and Sue Weitner

In December 1972, before the renovation was to be presented to the membership for approval, Stein was nominated for an unprecedented fourth (year) term. The Nominating Committee Report, in providing its reasoning, stated:

> Everyone spoke about the great improvement of the Club, the use of the Club, and the upgrading of the Club's facilities since Don assumed the position of President. It is a "crushing" reward that three years of service be succeeded by a fourth year. However, the Club is in a transitional period and the Committee felt that Don's experience would be invaluable.

The following spring, Chairman Goldman sought a cost estimate for the overall project from J.E. Dunn Construction which he projected to be $1,500,000 plus $250,000 for golf course improvements, which he rounded up to a total of $1,800,000. Board member Paul Uhlmann, who had delivered the foregoing Nominating Committee report, suggested it would be advisable to scale down the plans to focus on new, expanded offices and a new bag storage room for between $300,000 and $400,000.

At a special meeting of the membership on April 29, 1973, architect Steve Abend showed slides of the proposed building remodel. Treasurer Bennett Levy projected that the additional space comprehended by the plans would result in additional operating costs of $27,000.

According to Abend and Ed Lapin, who served on the board at the time, the plans included handball courts. The Jewish Community Center, which was then located between Troost and Holmes not far from Oakwood, had them, and many existing and "prospective" members played handball.

Approval of the entire plan including a proposed dues increase of $29 per month and a new loan of $1,720,000 was declined by the membership. Subsequently, the Building Committee reported that a survey of the membership indicated that while they were in favor of the "new facilities," they were unwilling to incur long-term indebtedness for it.

Eight years later, under President Leonard Rose, a somewhat less elaborate plan which would have been financed by a five-year, $50 per month assessment was also not approved. At that point, no significant capital improvement projects were to be proposed until the early 2000s.

When asked what he viewed as turning points in the club's history, Bill Fromm pointed to the failure to approve the improvement plans during Don Stein's term and the admission of Jews into Kansas City's top-tier country clubs.

OAKWOOD FAMILY MEMORIES —
Love and Wang families

By Missy Love

My earliest childhood memories are of all the great times we had at Oakwood. Summers were filled with swimming and hanging out at OCC. I was on both the swim and tennis teams my whole life growing up.

My sixteenth birthday party was also at the club. It was a very special night filled with music and dinner. I was on swim team with Rob Klein, who had a band at the time, and his band played at my party. I can't remember the name of the band, but it was a lot of fun.

In talking to my family, my grandmother Sarah Wang and grandparents Bertha and Sol Silberg were longtime members of the club. My dad, Myron Wang, has also been a member for 67 years, since 1955. He married my mother, Marsha Pachter, at the club in 1962.

Later in life, Bill and I joined Oakwood in 2005. We were just dating when we joined because he was a man without a golf club at the time. He has played in the Saturday Game for the past 17 years. It was great reacquainting myself with many of my childhood friends and families that I grew up with. We love being a part of this rebirth that Oakwood has had and sharing this with so many people who have longtime affiliations with Oakwood like myself. I have so many great memories and so much pride when we bring guests out to the "new Oakwood."

Extended Wang Family at wedding of Missy Wang and Bill Love, 2007

President Stan House, left, and Tom Watson cutting the ribbon to the new holes, April 1993

CHAPTER 8

The Growth Years— 1980 to 1999

The 1980s and 1990s were a time of growth and expansion of various activities at Oakwood.

The 1980s started with a bang as Oakwood celebrated its centennial with a Century Ball, a black-tie gala. Among those who served on the committee planning the ball included longtime members Paul Uhlmann, Ed Kander, and Ruthie and Harold Tivol. Oakwood member and Kansas City Mayor Richard Berkley issued a proclamation honoring the milestone.

The Century Ball was a lavish affair with American Beauty red roses spread throughout the clubhouse and historic photos dotting each table. The Gold rooms were converted into a 19th century dance hall with performers Dorothy Coulter and Brian Steele providing the entertainment. A crowd of 270 attended the celebratory event, each receiving a parchment paper booklet with a history of Oakwood penned by Ken Krakauer.

Oakwood continued to be the social hub for many Jewish families. According to Krakauer, Oakwood was less family oriented at the beginning of the 1980s than it is today. In fact, several young

Invitation and program to the President's Ball, 1998

families of long-standing membership took leave of Oakwood as they approached the age of 35 and the resultant increase in dues. However, most of them returned in subsequent years with the requirement that they pay the lesser of an initiation fee or the dues that were avoided during their absence.

One element remained steadfast—Oakwood's sterling reputation for serving wonderful food. Chef Mike Storm, coming from a restaurant family, started as executive chef in 1993. While Oakwood's membership rolls were full, leaders kept a close eye on the numbers as country club membership overall began to dip near the end of the 1990s. Despite those concerns, Oakwood underwent almost continuous upgrading to its physical plant and expansion of its activities for children and women during these two decades.

Leisure Sports and Recreation

Whether participating in Oakwood's camp or enjoying the pool, tennis courts, golf course, or the on-site lake on their own, many kids spent their summer break at the club enjoying its amenities. Yet there were protocols for behavior.

"There were definite rules for kids and adults," Jenny Isenberg said. "Kids would never think about going to the bar or other places upstairs without being properly dressed."

Many memories were made during the summer months.

"There was something special about growing up at Oakwood and the magic of summers there," said Jack Greenbaum.

"I remember being young, probably six or seven, and going fishing with my mom and a friend at the lake on the Oakwood golf course," Greenbaum said. "It was tranquil standing out on the dock with the poles in the water. Suddenly, I felt a tug on my line and started reeling in something big; after a while, I handed the rod over to my mom and to my friend, and we're all taking turns. Finally, as the line drew closer to the dock, we peered over to see what I caught. Lo and behold a snapping turtle is on the end of the line—and it's angry! We panicked and rushed to get one of the greenskeepers who was able to cut the line, releasing the turtle," Greenbaum said. "That about ended my fishing career."

Jonathan Jacobs has fond memories of summertime at Oakwood.

"I remember trying to be the first one in the pool the day it opened each year and hiding in lockers, sneaking into the men's locker room or upstairs where it is old and creepy," Jacobs said. "There was something special about growing up at Oakwood and the magic of summers there. Oakwood was a home away from home for me from a very young age and still to this day," Jacobs said.

Golf

Golf continued to be the dominant sport at Oakwood. The Missouri Men's Golf Championship was held for the first time at Oakwood in 1986 and won by Don Bliss of St. Louis.

Golf leadership also experienced changes. Golf pro Hermie Scharlau retired after a long tenure with Oakwood. Scharlau taught several generations of children how to play the game.

"I can still feel Hermie Scharlau's calloused hands over mine, helping me to learn," Jenny Isenberg said.

Billy Peterson took over the pro position from Hermie Scharlau in 1982 and stayed until resigning in 1988 to take the position at Hallbrook Country Club. Bill Baraban stepped into the role until 1997 when he left to move to Atlanta for a head position at the Standard Club. J.R. Rotarius served as Oakwood's golf pro from 1997–2000.

Women's golf continued to grow with the Country Club District Women's Golf Association

HERMIE SCHARLAU TEES OFF FOR NEW CAREER

In recognition of Hermie Scharlau's years of service as a golf professional, we have compiled a score of photographs to recap his dedication to golf and friends.

The front of Hermie Scharlau's retirement brochure, 1982

TOM WATSON AND OAKWOOD

Tom Watson's connections to Oakwood go back to his teen years as a member of the Kansas City Golf Association's junior program.

"I remember going to play in a junior event on a Monday," Watson said. "I was probably about 10, and I remember the golf course, and the first couple of holes were short so anyone who was a young golfer could hit a birdie. ... Later on, I played in the Kansas City Men's Match play, and I think I was 17 and I won it."

Watson married Linda Rubin in Oakwood's Blue Room. Over the years, Watson played at Oakwood frequently with his father-in-law, Irving Rubin.

"He was one of the greatest human beings I ever met," said Watson of Rubin, "but he wasn't much of a golfer."

Watson also played with his brother-in-law and then-manager Chuck Rubin. Watson would also play with longtime club pro Hermie Scharlau.

"Hermie, Chuck, and I would go out in the middle of the summer, and it was hot, and no one was out there, and we would play," Watson recalled. Over the years, Watson developed a friendship with Scharlau and his wife, Dottie.

"Both were characters, and over the years, I got to know them very well. I spent a number of winters down in Florida with Herman getting ready for the tour. He taught the game as a passion."

Watson's son, Michael, and daughter, Meg, attended summer camp at Oakwood. There were other outings with his kids at Oakwood.

"I remember one episode of taking my son out to the lake to fish on the sixth hole," Watson said. "He was learning to cast, and I looked away and I heard a 'kaboosh' and he stepped into the lake," said Watson with a laugh. "I've had great times out at Oakwood."

Club member (and caddy) Aaron Garry and Tom Watson

inviting Oakwood women to participate in its activities. Member Lynn Poskin was part of the team that won the Ladies Championship in 1998. Poskin played a pivotal role in the evolution of women's golf at Oakwood.

"We applied to get into this district for competitive golf with other clubs," Poskin said. "It helped me to become a better golfer."

Competition for the coveted KC Cup in women's golf began in the 1990s, and Poskin led the charge to win it. Oakwood was successful in that pursuit in the mid-2000s, taking second place.

Arnold Palmer played in an exhibition at Oakwood in 1982.

Oakwood played host to the first American Junior Golf Association tournament in Kansas City. More than 100 teens—both boys and girls—participated in the stroke-play competition. From that point on, Oakwood was part of a regular rotation of clubs for the event.

Arnold Palmer prepares an iron shot from the tee.

Arnold Palmer takes a swing during an exhibition in 1982.

Swimming

Oakwood's competitive swimming program continued to grow by leaps and bounds. Lynn Poskin was also instrumental in the growth of the swim team with her own children participating.

"When our kids were swimming, we urged the club to get out of the league we were in and get us into the country club swim league, and it was a big deal," Poskin said.

"I remember the relay team of Chandler Hampton, Becky Poskin, Hannah Bock, and Abby Grossman got first place in the city championships in the 1980s—the only Oakwood relay team to do that," Poskin said.

Jonathan Jacobs was a member of the swim team for a number of years.

"Swim meets were really fun," Jacobs said. "But one day, I really didn't want to partake in swim practice (because) it was cold outside, and the water was even colder. So, I purchased a Baby Ruth candy bar from the snack bar and tossed it in the deep end when no one was watching. I made sure to point it out to the lifeguard and just like that, practice was canceled so they could shock the pool with chlorine and remove the candy bar that so accurately displayed itself as poop."

Oakwood's swim team participated in various meets throughout the city with many parents helping at the competitions.

"The parents worked so hard to make sure everything went beautifully," Poskin said. During Poskin's involvement with the swim teams, two Oakwood swimmers won the prestigious "Wally E. Daniels Memorial Award" given by the Country Club Swim Association of Kansas City to a youth club member for sportsmanship.

In 1999, Oakwood hosted the Country Club Swim Championships with more than 1,500 swimmers competing over the three-day event.

Club Operations

The club's leadership focused on making changes to various governance policies during the 1980s, including creation of a permanent capital improvement and replacement fund. Various assessments were instituted and continued through the 1990s to cover numerous renovations.

Club manager Hans Weyh served from 1970 to 1992.

For more than a century, Oakwood was governed by men only. That policy changed when Eileen Cohen became the first woman to serve as a board member, although she was not allowed to vote. That policy was later modified, giving women the right to vote on club matters.

Lynn Poskin, whose father, Jerry Epstein, had served on the board, was also one of the women who pushed for the changes.

"When we graduated from college, my sister and I went to the board and appealed for the legacy membership that was offered to me be changed and offered to other women as well, and they did," Poskin said. She would later take a leadership role serving as an Oakwood board member and later as the second woman president of the club. Over the years, Poskin's family has left its mark on Oakwood's leadership; both of her parents, her husband, brother, sister, and sister-in-law have all served as board members and on various committees.

KANSAS CITY HISTORY TIMELINE

Kansas City began the decade of the 1980s with an intensive heat wave of 17 consecutive 100-degree-plus days. In the 1990s, climatological changes caused heavy rains, flooding more than 600 homes and 102 businesses along the Blue River. Additional flooding took place as a result of a pattern of drought followed by intense rain.

The community was left in shock when 114 people died and 216 were injured in the collapse of the Hyatt Hotel's Skywalks during a summer tea dance. Six Kansas City firefighters died fighting a blaze from an explosion at a southside construction site.

The business arena had its share of mergers, acquisitions, and bankruptcies. Real estate firm Kroh Brothers went bankrupt. Sprint was born from the merger of United Telecommunications and GTE Corporation with its world headquarters located in Overland Park. Both Missouri and Kansas started lotteries, Kansas approved liquor by the drink, and the Woodlands started business for dog and horse racing. The metro's first casino opened in nearby Riverside. Bartle Hall expanded, and the American Royal Arena complex was completed.

Legal troubles plagued several Kansas Citians. Financier Frank Morgan, who helped build Kansas City's skyline, faced legal troubles throughout these decades. The Argent Skimming Trial resulted in the convictions of several Kansas City mob leaders for skimming funds from a Las Vegas hotel and casino. Four Kansas City Royals players pled guilty to cocaine charges. The U.S. Supreme Court declared the Kansas City School District desegregation plan too excessive. Local leaders closed schools and cut costs.

In the political world, Rev. Emanuel Cleaver became the first African American mayor of Kansas City, following the first Jewish mayor, Richard Berkley. By 1999, Kansas Citians elected their first woman mayor, Kay Waldo Barnes. Voters approved a metro-wide 911 network as well as a bi-state tax to restore Union Station.

The Kansas City Royals won the World Series in 1985. Ewing Kauffman, the Royals owner and founder of Marion Laboratories, passed away in 1993. It would take the Royals another 50 years to win the title again after several ownership changes.

In the arts world, The Kansas City Philharmonic closed its doors, but banker Crosby Kemper came to the rescue, starting the Kansas City Symphony. Pop star Michael Jackson began his World Victory Tour with three concerts at Arrowhead Stadium. The Kansas City Jazz Museum opened in the historic 18th & Vine District.

(Excerpted from Kansas City: An American History *by Rick Montgomery and Shirl Kasper, Kansas City Star Books, 2007.)*

In 1991, Oakwood entered into a reciprocal privileges' agreement with Meadowbrook Country Club, located across the state line in Prairie Village, Kansas. More centrally located, Meadowbrook offered many Oakwood members closer proximity to playing a game of golf, using its large swimming pool, and grabbing a meal in its dining room.

During the 1980s and 1990s, several members moved through the office of board president including Frank Hoffman, Harold Tivol, Bennett "Bud" Levy, Melvin Krigel, and Stan Goldberg. By 1992, longtime Oakwood member Stan House succeeded Goldberg.

"I installed myself because Stan [Goldberg] had fallen and broken his leg and couldn't make the installation," House recalled.

Under his leadership, House put several operational changes in place.

"I was the first one to put in a food minimum for the club and the first to have monthly newsletters, which had not been done before," he said.

House's tenure as board president was productive, but there was the occasional encounter with members disgruntled about some aspect of operations. House said he was polite in his encounters with members whether in the dining room or on the golf course.

"One time I was on the first tee ready to play golf, and someone came up with a hamburger to complain about something and I said, 'As soon as I'm done, I will be happy to help you with your hamburger problem,'" House said.

"One member complained that we only had soft rolls, and he wanted to have hard rolls too, and I jokingly told him we would never have hard rolls under my presidency," House said. Irwin Blond, Jim Greenwood, and Ward Katz served as presidents finishing out the 1990s.

In 1997, the board unveiled its long-range planning project, Vision 2000. The project achieved many significant changes to the club under presidents Jim Greenwood and Ward Katz. A new social membership category was added to boost membership rolls. When Katz became club president in 1998, the board proposed and the membership approved a bylaw amendment granting equal rights for spouses, giving them the opportunity to vote, and serve as board members and officers of the club.

Club management changed several times during these two decades. After 22 years as club manager, Hans Weyh retired, passing the torch to Claudio Caviglia, who served until 2001 when Gerald King became club manager.

Whether preparing 400 meals for the Fourth of July buffet or a delicious lobster dinner for a private party, Oakwood's culinary reputation continued to soar despite the management changes. In the culinary department, Kansas City native Mike Storm returned from Topeka in 1993 to become Oakwood's executive chef. Storm remains as Chef Emeritus today, 30 years later, helping to enhance Oakwood's already stellar reputation for its culinary offerings.

Oakwood has always been known for its excellent food.

EXCLUSION OF JEWS FROM KANSAS CITY COUNTRY CLUBS

The raison d'être of the Progress Club and, later, Oakwood Country Club, was to offer opportunities for social interaction and sports for members of the Jewish community.

It was a known fact that from the 1880s, when the Progress Club was founded, through the 1960s, Jews were not permitted in several of the more prestigious social or business clubs in Kansas City. The same also held true for country clubs through the 1980s. This was a contributing factor to Oakwood's success.

However, things began to change for country clubs around 1990. Then, civic and business leader Henry W. Bloch, one of the founders and the chief executive of H&R Block, Inc.—and also a member of Oakwood—was proposed for membership at the Kansas City Country Club. In November 1990, *The Kansas City Star* reported that Bloch's application was withdrawn by the "proposer" and never reached the board of directors.

This obvious exclusion may not have become a cause célèbre had world-renowned professional golfer Tom Watson, himself a member of the Kansas City Country Club, not resigned in protest. Shortly thereafter, Bloch was admitted.

While it is not clear whether Bloch was the first Jew to be admitted to one of the top-tier non-Jewish country clubs in the Kansas City area, it clearly signaled that the game had changed, and it became fairly commonplace for members of Oakwood to join other clubs.

While not all Oakwood members who joined other clubs resigned from Oakwood, many did, and other members of the Jewish community chose to join clubs other than Oakwood.

Incidentally, Tom Watson, who had been married to Linda Rubin—whose family were Oakwood members—was an honorary member of Oakwood for many years.

A corollary to the exclusion of Jews from other country clubs in the Kansas City area is whether non-Jews could become members of Oakwood. A review of governing documents revealed no such policy, and a survey of several older members who were in leadership positions indicates there was never such a policy. In fact, at the March 1969 meeting of the board of directors with Jack Reitzes presiding, a resolution affirming Oakwood's policy of non-discrimination was passed.

However, as indicated above, Oakwood was known as a Jewish club, and it would not be unusual for people in the greater community to ask "is Oakwood still a Jewish club?" While the answer was clearly that it was not exclusively a Jewish club, the reality was that, other than some non-Jewish spouses of members or members' children, there were few if any non-Jewish members until late in the twentieth century.

Lenny Hershman, who was the membership chairman in the early 1980s, reflects that occasionally someone who clearly was not Jewish would inquire about membership and would be referred to Hershman, who would explain the application and approval process. That process required every applicant to have a sponsor and three personal references. While not intended to purposefully exclude a non-Jew from membership, this practice may have had that effect. However, as the years progressed and Jews were admitted to other clubs, Oakwood had an increasing number of non-Jewish members.

For golf course management, Oakwood hired Jeff Elmer as golf course superintendent in 1996 following Gil Collins's retirement. Over a span of 75 years, many of Elmer's family worked at Oakwood.

Renovations

In addition to policy and management changes, Oakwood's physical plant underwent numerous changes. An ice storm in 1983 destroyed the old Bermuda section of some fairways on the golf course. The club seized the opportunity to replace these with zoysia stripping that started a continuous process of improvements to the course.

Golf legend Tom Watson was instrumental in the redesign of several holes on the Oakwood course including the fifth hole, notorious for the hilly terrain.

At Watson's suggestion, Oakwood leadership hired golf architect Scott Miller to create a master plan to renovate the course.

"They came to me and asked if I would design it [the fifth hole] and I said 'sure,'" Watson said. "I just changed the right side of the green. I also gave advice on the sixth hole to make it a more 'fair' shot, by adding a bunker," he said. "I think Herman [Scharlau] agreed with me."

On May 3, 1992, Oakwood held a dedication ceremony when the first phase of renovations was complete. Watson was on hand for the occasion, taking part in an exhibition with Oakwood Golf Pro Bill Baraban. Watson was pleased with the changes made to the sixth hole.

"Fortunately, I didn't bunker when we opened it," said Watson with a chuckle.

In 1993, work on the 10th, 15th, and 16th holes

Dedication of the new holes in 1992. Tom Watson discusses strategy with Oakwood pro Bill Baraban.

President Stan House and long-time member and Oakwood historian Ken Krakauer at the dedication of the new holes in 1992.

was completed. By 1997, five new greens designed by golf architect Craig Schreiner were opened for play, and a new practice range became operational.

Elmer, who had replaced Gil Collins after his retirement, took responsibility for the course and worked with Schreiner to prepare the new greens at the first, second, third, 15th, and 17th holes.

Beginning in 1986, the clubhouse experienced a facelift with improvements to the east end of the clubhouse, including a halfway house with a food-and-beverage facility. The results provided close proximity to restrooms for golfers and others, and more storage space for food service equipment.

With various renovations in place, a number of families used Oakwood for important family life-cycle events.

"I was married at Oakwood on Sunday afternoon," Jenny Isenberg said. "I went out to Oakwood early, and I swam laps by myself. It was like my own private mansion."

John and Jenny Isenberg's wedding at Oakwood with attendants Lynn Epstein Poskin and Tom Isenberg

Years later, Isenberg's daughter Allison was also married at Oakwood.

Near the end of the 1980s, plans were being completed for a new, larger swimming pool so Oakwood's young swimmers could continue to compete against the swim teams at other local clubs. The new Olympic-sized, six-lane pool opened in 1991, much to the delight of Oakwood's competitive swim team and those who enjoyed a leisurely dip on a hot summer day. More golf cart storage was a welcome addition as well.

Into the 1990s, Oakwood received a new front entrance, club offices were expanded, and additional areas were made accessible to persons with disabilities. The club designated a no-smoking grill although smoking was still permitted in a number of areas including the cocktail lounge and the Blue Room. The club also installed cable TV in the lounge areas, which proved to be a big hit with golfers and sports fans. Renovations were made to the Gold rooms as well as the main dining room, providing more opportunities for private parties.

In the mid-1990s, the board approved the remodeling of the Blue Room, located at the east end of the building. Steve Block and Ward Katz co-chaired the committee to oversee the remodeling. Upon completion, it was renamed the Progress Room, a nod to the club's original name.

Tennis players were pleased with various improvements including a clubhouse and restroom facility, which also served campers in the summer months. A covered area was created to accommodate campers for food service and activities.

By the end of the 1980s, Oakwood's membership rolls were full, with over 675 members of all classifications. Yet in the 1990s, the membership roster began a slow but steady decline that would ultimately change the future of Oakwood. Longtime member Bill Fromm had his own take on membership's downward trend.

"When other KC clubs (non-Jewish) started to admit Jewish members [including Meadowbrook in the late 1970s], it was a great turn of events for the Jewish and non-Jewish community, but a terrible turn of events for Oakwood, because now people had an alternative that wasn't stuck out in the southeast corner of the city," Fromm said. "That was the beginning of the decline of Oakwood Country Club, when Jews started to have alternatives."

Under President Jim Greenwood, in anticipation of the millennium, the board adopted a long-range plan entitled Vision 2000 which included many policy changes to modernize the club. It contemplated the adoption of these changes over time.

In 1999, the first American Junior Golf Association tournament ever in the Kansas City area was held at Oakwood. The club was the original site as part of a rotation among the better private clubs in the area. About 100 boys and girls under college age from throughout the country came for a stroke-play competition. Also in 1999, Oakwood hosted the Country Club Swim Championships. With 1,500 swimmers competing each day for three consecutive days, Oakwood had a chance to shine for thousands of Kansas City-area club members.

Toward the end of the decade and for several years thereafter, there were efforts to encourage Meadowbrook to consider merging the two clubs. The principal stumbling block was that while Oakwood had the superior golf course, Meadowbrook's location was superior. Meadowbrook also had a debt level that was an obstacle. Finally, some believed that certain descendants of the original members of Meadowbrook, which was founded in the early 1950s, harbored resentment toward Oakwood, which was founded 70 years earlier by German Jews and that, for many years, Eastern European Jews may not have been welcomed. However, there is no available evidence to support this.

OAKWOOD FAMILY MEMORIES —
The Bogey Bums

by Merilyn Berenbom and Joel Goldman

(Part of the extended Krigel-Tivol-Goldman-Berenbom-Maslan Families)

THE BOGEY BUMS ARE AN ETERNAL OAKWOOD LEGACY

Established in the 1960s, the group consisted of thirteen couples: Ruthie and Herb Krigel, Marsha and Jules Goldman, Buddy and Joyce Greenbaum, Sevi and Mel Krigel, Marjorie and Jules Kantor, Paula and Ralph Zarr, Thelma and Paul Byers, Lionel and Kay Greenberg, Meriel and Stan Winn, Connie and Jack Reitzes, and Eloise and Julius Minkoff.

The Bogey Bums were a golf group whose games were consistently inconsistent. Their golf games (and the commentary) could have been entertaining in and of themselves. The collective sense of humor of this group went far beyond the golf course.

Each year, an "Idol" was chosen among the Bogey Bums by a top-secret process. The Idol expected to be put on a pedestal and worshipped accordingly. In fact, though, the Idol was in charge of planning parties. These parties defied imagination. Clues for an upcoming party could be found in the want ads of *The Kansas City Star* or in a lockbox at Union Station. The Bums were known for fantastic fun.

Another task of the Idol was to provide a blue tee to each Bum on the first hole. This was called getting a bluey from your Idol.

The wives of the Bums were known as the Bogey Broads. The children proudly accepted their title, Bogey Brats.

Over the decades, the Broads became the party planners. Every simcha was celebrated.

This amazing group of people was far more than a golf group. While they defined the power of joy and laughter, they also defined the power of strength and compassion in the most trying of times.

They were there for each other through illnesses and deaths that came too early. Their collective kindness, smiles, extended hearts and hands live on.

Bogey Bums, from left, Lionel Greenberg, Stan Winn, Jack Reitzes, Jules Kantot, and Ralph Zarr

Ralph Zarr and the Bogey Broads

The winners each week put a certain amount of money in the kitty. The losers put in more. At the end of the season, they used the money for a group trip or a party.

The amazing thing is that the Bogey Bums left a legacy of fun and love that resonates today. Not everyone could be a Bogey Bum but everyone wished they could.

Since Ken Block and his ownership group took control of Oakwood, many improvements have been made to the club as well as adding new amenities.

CHAPTER 9
Oakwood Embraces a New Future

Following up on Vision 2000, Oakwood President Ward Katz (1998–2001) implemented several changes, including revisions to the bylaws codifying initiatives previously proposed and adopted piece-meal. These included enabling women to have equal membership rights as men; providing married couples two equal votes; and permitting women to serve as club officers and directors. A new class of social membership was established, and a food and beverage minimum was instituted. The same year, The Dedicated Tree program was inaugurated. The Country Club District Women's Golf Association invited Oakwood women to participate. In addition, the board created a long-range capital improvement plan with the help of a golf club consultant, The McMahon Group. Several proposals were presented to the membership for discussion at a series of meetings. However, with a change in management occasioned by the resignation of manager Claudio Caviglia and an accounting error resulting in a larger than anticipated operating assessment, the entire effort was tabled. Leadership would wait to move forward.

With help from member Bob Bernstein's firm, Bernstein Rein, Oakwood adopted a new logo, a stylized oak leaf, which continues to the present. New steel tee markers incorporating the new logo were purchased and installed by greens superintendent Jeff Elmer.

Oakwood golf hat with stylized Oakleaf logo designed by Bernstein Rein

Golf continued to take center stage at Oakwood. In 1999, Oakwood hosted The Wood Cup, a Ryder Cup-style golf tournament, between Oakwood and Westwood Country Club in St. Louis. Katz and his law school classmate and good friend, Harold Sarner, who served as Westwood's president at the same time Katz was Oakwood's president, conceived the tournament. Westwood hosted the first Wood Cup, which it won. Oakwood hosted the following year and took the prize. The Wood Cup was played eight times between 1999 and 2014. The final match was played in St. Louis, where the Cup currently resides. In addition to Katz, Oakwood players who competed over the years included Jeff Brick, Robert Cohen, Andy Kaufman, Peter Shapiro, Andy Epstein, Robert Turtledove, David Shapiro, Bob Bushman, Jim Greenwood, and Bill Koenigsdorf. Women, including Donna Katz, Kay Johnson, and Jill Shapiro, also competed for several years.

In 2000, Oakwood was honored to host the Missouri Golf Association's leading event, the Match Play Championship. About 150 of Missouri's best male golfers participated. Bert Benjamin won the tournament, being the first and only Oakwood player to win it in five decades.

Jim Farrell, who had been assistant golf pro, succeeded Joe Rotarius as the head golf pro. New and existing golf programs blossomed, including member-guest events the Acorn Classic and the Knickerbocker, the Susan G. Komen Breast Cancer Fundraising tournament, Junior Golf, and the Women's Interclub League. Oakwood teams also competed in the men's Interclub League.

During the balance of 2000 and into 2001, the club made vigorous efforts to improve its staff and its bottom line, achieving a break-even year. Under President David Goodman (2001–2002), the board revisited the 2000 proposed capital program recommendation. The membership approved spending

Oakwood golfer Jeff Brick and Westwood Country Club of St. Louis golfer David Lipsitz at the Wood Cup, 2000

KANSAS CITY HISTORY TIMELINE

Entering the new millennium, the Kansas City SmartPort, a non-profit, investor-based organization, was established to attract logistics investments in the metro area. Growth continued in many areas of the metro including the 2007 opening of the Sprint Center, now the T-Mobile Center, a multi-purpose arena in the heart of Downtown Kansas City. The arena hosts major sports events including the Big 12 basketball tournament as well as major celebrity concerts drawing thousands from across the country.

Other changes to Kansas City's landscape included the Kauffman Center for the Performing Arts (2011) designed by noted architect Moshe Safdie. The center is home to several arts organizations, including the Kansas City Symphony, as well as concerts, lectures, and more. Other places went through major renovations including Arrowhead and Kauffman stadiums. Out in Johnson County, additional youth soccer fields were added through the Johnson County Park and Recreation District accommodating the increased demand. The county continued its efforts to add more parks in the community.

Redevelopment took place in Wyandotte County with the opening of the Kansas Speedway racetrack and a new stadium for professional soccer, Children's Mercy Park; retail, restaurants, and hotels sprang up to support NASCAR. Residential growth continued in the suburbs both north and south of Kansas City; by 2022 the Kansas City Metro Region had grown to nearly 2.4 million.

Additional enhancements to the entertainment sector were the Power and Light District—adjacent to the T-Mobile Center—and the opening of Legoland Discovery Center Kansas City and Sealife at Crown Center. Kansas City's Zoo has continued to grow with an aquarium opening in 2023.

One Kansas City landmark, the Liberty Memorial, was thrust into the spotlight with its 2014 designation as the National World War I Museum and Memorial.

Kansas City sports fans had plenty to smile about as the Kansas City Chiefs finally returned to the Super Bowl after a 50-year drought, winning the title in 2020, 2023, and again in 2024. The Kansas City Royals also returned to the world stage after a half century winning a second World Series title in 2015. Professional hockey hit the scene with the 2009 arrival of the Kansas City Mavericks hockey team. Another professional baseball team, The T-Bones, changed owners and names, becoming the Kansas City Monarchs—an homage to the Negro Leagues team of earlier decades. Men's professional soccer continued changing both ownership and names, the most recent being Sporting KC, which won the MLS Cup in 2013 (the previous team won in 2000). Women's professional soccer came on the scene with the latest iteration being the Kansas City Current. It began play as an expansion team in the National Women's Soccer League in 2021 with a new stadium under construction on the riverfront.

> In the political world, several mayors ruled Kansas City each with their own leadership style including Kay Barnes, Mark Funkhouser, Sly James, and Quinton Lucas.
>
> The late 2000s saw Kansas City coping with racial protests following the George Floyd murder and calls for changes within the Kansas City Missouri Police Department. The metro also experienced the Covid-19 pandemic, forcing many businesses and municipalities to shutter operations sending people to work from home. Schools went virtual as many worked from home. Once the pandemic wave began to subside toward the end 2022, schools and many businesses returned to in-person status; however, remote work remained an option and some safety precautions remained in place.

$1.5 million to cover the replacement of the golf course irrigation system with a new, three-row system and computerized pumping station. The remodeling of the bar and lounge also proceeded, with the addition of an outside deck off the bar. The club dedicated these improvements in 2002.

Member John Uhlmann was simply "following in the footsteps of his family" when he personally funded the design and construction of the golf short game facility in 2003, located beyond the south end of the driving range. John wanted to thank prior generations of club members—including his own family—and enhance the club for future members. John Uhlmann's grandfather, Paul Uhlmann Sr., had been club president in 1936 and 1937. Pat Uhlmann, John's father, started a tree farm to beautify the golf course along the 11th hole.

Under President Jeff Rosen (2003 to 2004), Kathy Brown, who had been an assistant to Gerald King, became the club's new general manager. Clubhouse improvements continued and, in 2004, expenditures of over $150,000 went toward myriad items to spruce up the club. The biggest expenses were for new banquet chairs, resurfacing the tennis courts, and new carpet in the grill, main dining, and Oakwood and Progress rooms.

In 2004, Jerry Miller became club president. Club leadership reined in spending in 2004 and 2005. In 2006, Oakwood added new chairs for card players in the west lounge and new ice machines for the halfway house and west lounge.

Highlighting Miller's term as president, the club celebrated its 125th anniversary with a spectacular gala—125 Magical Years—held on September 16, 2006. The club's driveway entry was adorned with 125 Year banners for the entire year.

The 125th Anniversary Ball program, 2006

Camp Oakwood also enjoyed a renaissance under outstanding member leadership with a marvelous curriculum of swimming, golf, tennis, art, drama, and music. Debbie Minkin succeeded Katie Marshall as camp director.

Junior Golfers in 2006

Dr. Jeff Brick succeeded Jerry Miller as president in 2007–2008. Brick had been the Greens and Grounds Committee chairman following longtime chair Dick Greenberg and said it was "his turn in the barrel" to serve as president. The major project that occurred during his term was the replacement of the old, deteriorated asphalt cart paths on the front nine (except part of the second hole) and the elimination of the asphalt cart paths on most of the back nine. With input from Chair Bill Koenigsdorf and the influence of the many golfers who preferred walking to riding, having cart paths only around tees and greens was adopted. Funds were lacking to complete paths on the back, but it was a vast improvement over the deteriorated and, in some cases, poorly located cart paths. Also, during that time, the club purchased push carts, which had previously been prohibited.

In 2013, a group of members contributed funds to reconstruct the gazebo located between the ninth green and 10th tees in memory of John Uhlmann. The gazebo was designed and the construction supervised by Kansas City architect Byron Emas.

Bill Koenigsdorf served as president from 2008 to 2010. Koenigsdorf was a stickler for rules and procedures that led to the cleanup of the bylaws. During Koenigsdorf's term, Chris Bancroft succeeded Kathy Brown as general manager. The parking lot, long in need of repair, was repaved and the cart path project was completed. For the first time in the club's history, the dining room was closed for part of the winter.

Bob Zeldin served as Oakwood's president from 2010–2012 followed by Polly Kramer, who was the club's first woman president as well as the first president who was a social member. Active with the Jewish Federation of Greater Kansas City, she was responsible for attracting a number of social members.

President Bob Zeldin and First Lady Jean Zeldin at Oakwood's 130th Anniversary Celebration, 2011

GOLF GROUPS

The history of Oakwood golf would be incomplete without mention of some of the many groups that played together for years. Golf groups, men and women, would form, expand, contract, and even merge as members died or were unable to continue playing golf. The golf groups became the mainstay of Oakwood golf, with members being lifelong friends and each group having stories, jokes, parties, annual award ceremonies, trips, and years of records of scores, "swords" and money exchanged in bets. Some of the groups played into the 2020s and are continuing to play. Following are some of the groups, including past players, and their regular days of play up to the present. Any groups not included are unintentional.

"THE FRIDAY GAME":
Ken Block, David Goodman, David Freirich, Bill Love, Mike Schultz, Mike Shteamer, Myron Haith, Steve Bresky, Bob Steer, Ward Katz, Vance Wentz, Curtis Yonke, David Orscheln, Anthony Knipp, Mark Taylor, Bob Steer, Lance Melber, and Rachel Carpenter.

"THE SATURDAY GAME":
Ken Block, David Goodman, David Freirich, Bill Love, Mike Schultz, Mike Shteamer, Myron Haith, Steve Bresky, Curtis Yonke, Vance Wentz, Jeff Rosen, John Jacobs, Gary Leifer, Ted Stein, Don Gessen, Steve Block, Andy Epstein, Irv Blond, Jeff Weiner, and Jim Greenwood.

WEDNESDAY AFTERNOON AND SATURDAY MORNING:
Bill Schifman, Buzzah Feingold, Lewis Nerman, Harvey Grossman, Ed Lapin, Juddy Johl, David Freirich, Craig Wilson, Jeff Weiner, and Tom Sight.

"THURSDAY NIGHT GOLF GROUP (TNGG)":
Wayne Auer, Bruce Blackman, John Hjalmarson, Bill Intrater, David Shapiro, Bob Tucci, Steve Katz, Robert Turtledove, Steve Ruben, Frank Sterneck, Frank Friedman, Mitchell Swartz, Eduardo Luckie, and Terry Bacsham.

THURSDAY AFTERNOON AND SUNDAY:
Gene Bortnick, Oscar Pinsker, Jack Fingersh, Gil Collins, and Cliff Trenton.

SATURDAY AND SUNDAY:
Richard Atlas, Joel Pelofsky, Howard Weiner, and Marc Bernstein.

SUNDAY:
Ward Katz, Bob Zeldin, Jeff Brick, Dan Scharf, Josh Garry, Harry Himmelstein, Mike Fishman, Harry Bosley, Jeff Dorfman, Jay Lubin, and Doug Stone.

"HARRY'S GAME" (SATURDAY):
Harry Himmelstein, Mike Rainen, Pete Levi, Herb Kohn, Irv Belzer, Ward Katz, Harry Bosley, Dan Scharf, and Mike Fishman.

THURSDAY AFTERNOON, SUNDAY MORNING, AND VARIOUS WEEKDAYS:
Joel Leibsohn, Jeff Brick, Mark Myron, Gary Leifer, Keith Novorr, Jim Klein, Gerry Reid, Doug Willhoite, and Joe Hiersteiner.

SATURDAY:
Lisa Block, Donna Katz, Phyllis Cohen, Lisa Lefkovitz, and Eileen Cohen.

SATURDAY:
Jerry Miller, Dan Scharf, Ronnie Goldsmith, Bob Levy, Jim Greenwood, Mike Fedotin, John Uhlmann, Bob Cohen, and Ward Katz.

THURSDAY AND SUNDAY:
Peter Shapiro, Andy Epstein, Robert Turtledove, Jeff House, Mike Ellis, Jeff Rosen, Don Swartz, and Mark Saper.

SATURDAY:
Frank Granatino, Jay McBride, Kyle Steinbrecher, Mike Wilson, Anthony Knipp, Alex Cuenca, Trevor Taylor, and Foss Mckay.

SATURDAY:
Doug Curry, Matt Streeter, Mike Adkins, Marc Loe, Brian Tornquist, Nate Sprague, Taylor Warwick, and Peyton Warwick.

OTHERS:
Sheldon Fleischman, Sudarshan Hebbar, Bill Koenigsdorf, Larry Greenbaum, Fred Greenbaum, Darren Selkus, Sanjaya Hebbar, Greg Soli, Joel Laner, and Mark Thornhill.

Bev Johl and Fran Brozman.

WEDNESDAY AFTERNOON:
Carol Freirich, Jill Shapiro, Barb Weiner, Linda Lyon, and Ronna Garry.

Bill Fromm, Ed Lapin, Lenny Hershman, Leonard Rose, Bart Cohen, Jack Brozman, Bert Benjamin, Tom Sight, and Buddy Soloff.

Rick Shteamer, Harvey Grossman, Bill Koenigsdorf, and Mike Shteamer.

Mark Cohen, Brad Freilich, David Porter, Steve Swartzman and Paul Fingersh.

The Saturday Game: Back row, from left, Bill Love, Mike Schultz, David Goodman, Mike Shteamer, Steve Block, Irv Blond, Jeff Rosen; front row, from left, Ken Block, Steve Bresky, David Freirich, Myron Haith, Andy Epstein.

Wednesday and Saturday Morning Golf Group: Back row, from left, Harvey Grossman, Juddy Johl, Jeff Weiner, Craig Wilson, Ed Lapin, Billy Schifman; front row, from left, Buzzah Feingold, Lewis Nerman, David Freirich.

Thursday Night Golf Group (TNGG): Back row, from left, David Shapiro, Bob Tucci, Steve Katz, Fred Seligson, Bruce Blackman, Steve Ruben, Bill Intrater; front row, from left: Wayne Auer, Frank Sterneck, John Hjalmarson.

Although not a golf group, an adjunct group consisting of the TNGG is the Thursday Night Ski Group (TNSG): front row, from left, Fred Seligson (kneeling), Jill Shapiro, Wayne Auer, Bill Intrater, John Hjalmarson; second row, from left, Bruce Blackman, Lisa Auer, Lynn Intrater, Steve Katz, Suzi Blackman, Cindy Tucci, Bob Tucci, Liz Hjalmarson; back row, from left, Ellen Katz, Cathy Seligson, David Shapiro.

Sudarshan Hebbar, Greg Soli, and others at Muirfield

By 2015, Mike Fishman became president and was confronted with dealing with major hail damage to the club's roof. With ingenuity and some good fortune, insurance proceeds were utilized to replace the entire original slate roof with new artificial slate material as well as new gutters. To pay for golf course equipment without requiring an assessment from the members, the club formed the Oakwood Eagles, in which members voluntarily contributed approximately $80,000 for the new equipment. With one boiler that had already failed, updates were made to the HVAC equipment, including decommissioning the old boilers before they fell apart.

Finally, the club started the process of completely remodeling both the ladies' and men's locker rooms, approving funds to make it happen. Locker room remodels had been studied on several occasions, but each time, unrealistic budgets prevented the project from moving forward. A committee including Fishman, Ward Katz, Lisa Auer, Bill Intrater, and architect Byron Emas came up with the idea of combining both the men's and women's locker rooms into the space occupied on the upper floor by the men's locker room, which had last been remodeled in the 1960s. Emas masterfully designed the locker rooms into attractive, useful space and value-engineered the project, which cost about $350,000, including all-new lockers.

A state-of-the-art driving range with a TrackMan system is part of the club's Center of Excellence initiative.

In 2016, following Fishman's administration, another Oakwood first occurred when a triumvirate was elected as an executive committee in lieu of a single president. Bob Tucci, Steve Katz, and Bill Intrater, all long-time members with different skills, shared the responsibility. During their tenure, the three men oversaw the completion of the new men's and women's locker rooms, including making the decision to replace the old lockers rather than just refacing them, and upgrading the bar with new seating arrangements and an open view of the pool and golf course. Under their leadership, the fitness room was repurposed to be a flex room for dinners, meetings, and some card games to take advantage of the views; the fitness equipment was moved into the west lounge to provide more exercise space.

After organizing a few focus groups to provide members a forum for communicating their vision for Oakwood, the Young Professionals Golf League was created. This weekly league gave about 20 of Oakwood's youngest members an opportunity to network and create new friendships to enhance their engagement at the club. But the biggest accomplishment was hosting the City Swim Championships. With a great volunteer turnout over a hot Kansas City weekend, Oakwood proved that, though small, it was a mighty club with an excellent staff and involved members. The championship committee was pleased with the results and supported holding the tournament again, which Oakwood's executive committee appreciatively but respectfully declined.

During the executive committee's tenure, it presented the membership with previously discussed potential solutions and new ones to address Oakwood's aging HVAC infrastructure.

When Lynn Poskin became president in 2017, the HVAC system finally got its facelift. Poskin had to deal with the resignation of Michael Charest as general manager. With the help of Vice President Bill Intrater, Poskin stepped in as the club's interim manager for several months while a search was undertaken for Charest's replacement.

"I had never run anything in my life," Poskin said. "It was a challenging time financially for the club."

Members voted at the annual meeting to buy a new HVAC system with money from a member-held limited liability corporation plus $100,000 assessed to the membership. Efforts began to form an LLC for Oakwood. With the LLC contract complete, work began on the HVAC installation. A new fountain was installed on the 16th hole. A successful Knickerbocker, Acorn Fourth of July, and outside tournaments filled the summer. However, problems persisted including a water main leak, which began in 2018. Sean Dougherty resigned to become the head golf professional of Blue Hills Country Club, and Chris Bussell came in for the 2018 golf season. The annual meeting was held and new bylaws, increased dues, and an assessment were approved.

In the 2018–2019 term, a Reinventing Oakwood Committee was formed to look for new ways to market the club, increase usage, and rethink its situation and future. The committee made plans to hire a new club pro, worked to repair or shut off water leaks, and engaged club benchmarking to help determine where the club stood among country clubs regarding assets and liabilities.

Staffing changes persisted during this era. Assistant golf professional Randy Shade was hired as head golf professional. Greens and grounds superintendent Nick Cray accepted his dream job back home. A committee was formed to hire Cray's successor, eventually choosing Brent Racer, who came in ready to work and continues to this day, picking up where Cray had left off and adding new improvements. A Sonic Solutions system was installed to eliminate algae in the big lake on the sixth hole.

Focused on recruiting new members, Oakwood launched a new, more user-friendly website.

In 2019, Aaron March was elected club president; he organized a strategic planning team and held several meetings to look toward Oakwood's future. New rules and regulations were introduced. The club welcomed another successful summer of tournaments. Meanwhile, board members were constantly meeting with outside clubs, organizations, companies, and others to help Oakwood chart its future.

The club held a midyear town hall meeting to discuss its future and midyear assessment. The board engaged Fairway Advisors Inc., and Oakwood was officially on the market, looking for capital investors or other solutions. At the annual meeting, membership approved the member group's proposition for the board to negotiate the sale of Oakwood.

March continued as president until April 30, 2020, when the club was sold to OCC Investors LLC, led by veteran Oakwood member Ken Block. The sale took place in the middle of the COVID-19 global pandemic. Despite the ownership change, Oakwood was a refuge for some members.

"You were outside, you could be with friends there and have a good time," David Goodman said. "COVID turned out to be a great thing for country clubs."

Since Block and his ownership group took control of Oakwood, many improvements have been made to the club as well as adding new amenities. New events and social gatherings have taken place. Oakwood was no longer considered "THE Jewish

The club's iconic bridge at the 18th Hole was dedicated in 2021 in memory of Oakwood member Steve Bresky.

club" but a club anyone could join. Yet, some Jewish touches remain.

"We still maintain some Jewish activities like Passover and Hanukkah dinners, but it has opened up to others as well," Goodman said.

"I think the turnaround of the club has been dramatic since Ken Block bought it," said long-time member Bill Fromm. "Kansas City's golfing community is over the top about what's going on at Oakwood."

For David Goodman, despite this new era for the club, Oakwood continues to be a special place.

"It's a big part of my life, and I have lots of friends out there. A lot of the guys I play golf with have been friends since my youth," Goodman said.

"Going out there makes me happy. It's like a second home. I just have a lot of new relatives I don't know yet."

For the next generation of members who grew up going to the club with their parents, Oakwood continues to be a favorite place to gather. Jonathan Jacobs fondly remembers swim meets as a kid, attending Bar and Bat Mitzvah parties as well as having his own wedding at Oakwood.

"I like to say that I became a member for golf, but I stay for the people," said Jacobs, who serves as the chair of Oakwood's social committee. "I have as much fun with the staff who are like friends as I do with the friends who are like family."

Putting Cottage and Putting Course completed 2023

Posing at the gate during the inaugural round of new holes #4 and #5, from left, Curtis Yonke, Lisa Block, Ken Block and Bob Steer

KEN BLOCK'S VISION FOR OAKWOOD

Kansas City real estate developer Ken Block has a reputation for creating first-class projects, whether office, industrial, medical, multifamily, or retail. His approach has been the same when he purchased Oakwood: crafting the very best country club with the finest golf course improvements, amenities, and services.

An astute businessman, Block knew the club had to be sold if it was to survive. Membership was significantly down and something had to change. The board of directors explored various ideas and put the club up for sale. Ultimately, the membership accepted Block's offer to purchase Oakwood.

"I wanted to give any member the chance to buy into the deal—there are about 40 people who are minority members," Block said. "They did it because they wanted to put money into something that was important to them."

Block decided to buy Oakwood for a number of reasons, both personal and professional.

"I had two friends, including Steve Bresky, who died, and a couple of other guys I knew died," Block said. Block's older brother and longtime Oakwood member Steve Block passed away in March 2023.

"A couple of close friends said, 'You need to enjoy the success that you've had before you aren't here.' That changed my view on a number of things, and this was one of them. I wanted to make sure that whatever we did, it would be pursuant to a long-term development plan that would create the finest golf and country club in the region. From a country club-type perspective, I wanted it to have the best facilities, so a social member would enjoy a host of amenities," he said.

For Block, buying Oakwood was more than just another business deal. Block's Oakwood roots run deep. His parents, Allen and Gloria Block, were married at Oakwood. Block rode the bus to camp at Oakwood where he learned to swim and golf and played tennis and ping pong.

"There were only so many things to do at Oakwood on a rainy day, but you had to find things to do and that's when you got into trouble," he said with a laugh.

As a teen, Block played in the Kansas City Junior Golf league with Pro Hermie Scharlau. "It was a lot of fun," Block recalled. "My parents forgot to pick me up once when we played at Swope Park, and I carried my clubs and walked home to 71st Street."

During his junior high and high school years, Block occasionally joined his father's Saturday game.

"You couldn't say anything. If you spoke, they thought the air would move and impact the game," he said.

After college and entering the "real" world of work, Block found Oakwood was the place to be. It was those first years out of college when Block received his own membership to Oakwood.

"When I went into business, there were a lot of people I was trying to do business with but had a hard time getting them to call me back. But at Oakwood, my dad would take me around to see them at the club and all of sudden I would get calls back," Block recalled. "The club was the center of influence. The beauty of the club was a lot of camaraderie, friendship, and business opportunities."

Once the club's sale was complete, Block and his team got to work. Oakwood is one of the oldest country clubs in Kansas City—it is on the National Register of Historic Places—and mixing old and new has been part of Block's development plan. While laser-focused on upgrading facilities and making additions to its amenities, Block has remained steadfast on keeping the architectural flavor of the club.

"Whatever we build out there, we made it look like the original Tudor design," Block said. "If you visit the club in two or three years, you're going to think all the improvements have been there forever."

One of the first changes under Block's ownership was making a policy change in membership, opening the club for all regardless of religious identification.

"When Passover comes, we celebrate Passover, and we had a big crowd in 2022," Block said. "When Easter comes, we celebrate Easter. We celebrate everything."

There are various membership options including weekday golfing, social, and full membership that include all of Oakwood's amenities. "The club is there for the members … you want to do something, do it."

Block and his membership group have been dedicated to making big changes at Oakwood. They have brought back old members and have added many, many new ones.

His philosophy on the project? "You don't do anything halfway; I only build Class A projects."

During the first year of ownership, early improvements included a new fitness center, sports bar, and upgrades to the bride and groom suites in a push for wedding bookings "to create a great experience," Block said.

Knowing that the golf course was a big draw for Oakwood, Block paid close attention to making major improvements.

New holes were added with water fountains and waterfalls.

"It's a dramatic change to the golf course and we built a brand-new range with TrackMan technology and a performance center with six bays, the latest tech, and a 2.5-acre short game course," Block said. "You can bring people from anywhere in the country to play. The facilities will never be closed and we will never shut them down," he said.

While a busy golf course, Oakwood continues to host a number of charity tournaments. Recently, *Golf Digest* recognized Oakwood's course as the third best golf-course transformation in the country.

During the second year under Block's ownership, work focused on creation of a performance center, pickleball courts, and improvements to the tennis courts. Future plans call for the addition of villas and cabins that can be purchased or rented.

"There's no club in this region that has all this. … It's unlike anything else. We are a tourist resort club but in the city," Block said.

Keeping that sense of community has been important in Block's vision for Oakwood. "I want to make sure we create a place where someone can have the same experience we had when we were little," he said. "It's a place to do business and we encourage young business people to do the same. I had people who mentored me, and I want to mentor people," Block said.

When Block took ownership in 2020, there was the perception that Oakwood was on the decline. "Now the perception is Oakwood is a unique quality development," Block said. "It has spurred on other clubs to make improvements."

"I think it is far beyond what they expected we would do," Block said. "I am creating a vision of Oakwood so that people around the country will know this club. … We want it to be a place that when people visit it, they walk away saying, 'That was fantastic!'"

OAKWOOD'S LONG-TERM EMPLOYEES

A club such as Oakwood, built on tradition, quality, and service, couldn't have survived as long as it has without many dedicated employees. Some became friends of members. Most of the long-term employees simply performed their jobs without fanfare but with dedication to the organization, its leadership, members, and their fellow employees.

Here is a list of many of them with their years of service, departments, and job titles. No doubt, some have been inadvertently left out and to them we apologize. However, if we receive information about them, we will post that information on the website accompanying this book.

Salad Chef Vera Taylor and Chef Mike Storm.

CURRENT

	DEPARTMENT	TITLE
Vera Taylor	Food & Beverage	Salad Chef
Mike Storm	Food & Beverage	Chef Emeritus
Brian Taylor	Food & Beverage	Line Chef
Katelyn Lawson	Administration	Assistant General Manager
Denise Wipperman	Administration	Administrative Assistant
John Martin	Golf Course	
Ryan Mosley	Golf Course	First Assistant Superintendent

PAST

20–25 YEARS	DEPARTMENT	TITLE
Nancy Williams	Administration	Accountant
Gil Collins	Golf Course	Course Superintendent
Hal Williams	Food & Beverage	Bartender
Jeff Elmer	Golf Course	Course Superintendent
Hans Weyh	Administration	General Manager
Cora Stone	House	Ladies Locker Attendant
Harold Sutton	Food & Beverage	Bartender
Ben Shaw	Food & Beverage	Sous Chef
Doris Weyh	Administration	Assistant Manager
Oscar Schnell	House	Clubhouse and Bar Manager
Lonnie Nelson	House	Porter

Name	Department	Title
Coopie Nelson	House	Locker Room Attendant
Edith Nelson	House	Locker Room Attendant, Waitress
Charlie Lewis	House	Locker Room Attendant
Ann Coleman	Food & Beverage	
Bunny Torpey	Golf	Head Golf Professional
Hermie Scharlau	Golf	Head Golf Professional
Dottie Scharlau	Golf	Assistant Golf Manager
Millie Robinson	Food & Beverage	

5–20 YEARS	DEPARTMENT	TITLE
Angie Mulhall	Food & Beverage	Director of Food & Beverage
Randy Shade	Golf	Director of Golf
Raymond Haynes	Food & Beverage	
Bill Ross	Pool	Pool Manager, Sports Camp Director
Willie Johnson	Food & Beverage	Cook
Nell Blaney	Food & Beverage	Waitress
Lily Gonzalez	Food & Beverage	Waitress
Wanda Watson	Administration	Accountant
Brian Smith	Food & Beverage	Waiter
Brian Jungden	Food & Beverage	Waiter
Tom O'Reilly	House	Maintenance
Gerrie Sanders	Food & Beverage	Waitress
Matthew Wagner	Food & Beverage	Waiter
John Williams	Food & Beverage	Sous Chef
Jim McAnany	Food & Beverage	Sous Chef
Cora McGinnis	Food & Beverage	Pantry Chef
Walter Tinner	Food & Beverage	Porter
Willie Mae Tinner	House	Locker Room Attendant
Ann Coleman	Food & Beverage	
Shawn Tinner	Food & Beverage	
Walter Tinner, Jr.	Food & Beverage	
J.B. Tinner	Food & Beverage	
Rodney Tinner	Food & Beverage	
Lonnie Nelson	Food & Beverage	
Shirley Williams	Food & Beverage	
Rene' Nelson	Food & Beverage	
Troy Witherington	Administration	Assistant Manager
Millie Robinson	Food & Beverage	Waitress, Card Attendant
Craig Spencer	Food & Beverage	Waiter

Name	Department	Position
Jerry Marrow	Food & Beverage	Waiter, Card Attendant
Steve Clark	Food & Beverage	Pastry Chef
Carla Jones	Food & Beverage	Waitress
Raymond Haynes	Food & Beverage	
Tim Hacker	Golf	Assistant Professional
Trisha Hacker	Food & Beverage	Dining Room Manager
Mr. Tucker	Food & Beverage	Banquet Manager
O.D.	Food & Beverage	Waiter, Banquet Manager
Jake Golding	Pool	Lifeguard
Tom Ruzicka	Pool	Lifeguard
Dave Kanter	Tennis	Tennis Pro
Sid Kanter	Tennis	Tennis Pro
Jake Hannas	Tennis	Tennis Pro
Scott Hull	Tennis	Tennis Pro
Don Robertson	Pool	Lifeguard
Brent Racer	Golf Course	Golf Course Superintendent
Jim Naudet	Golf Course	Assistant Golf Superintendent
Bob Griffin	Golf Course	Mechanic
Mark Rooney	Golf Course	Assistant
Roger Wilkens	Golf Course	Mechanic
Delbert McGuire	Golf Course	Operator
Tom Naudet	Golf Course	Crew Member
Paul Naudet	Golf Course	Crew Member

OAKWOOD FAMILY MEMORIES —
Grossman and Zeldin families

by Jean Zeldin

One of my early childhood memories is being part of a children's "chorus," singing "99 Bottles of Beer on the Wall" at the top of our lungs on the bus that drove us to and from Oakwood Day Camp. "SO(south)-5501" was one of the first phone numbers I learned because I could find my parents there on most Saturday nights. It was a given for many years that New Year's Eve meant a party at "The Club." The number 192 was my father's club number. (Women were not considered members back then.)

As a teenager, I hung out at Oakwood, swam, and played golf there. So many of my childhood and adult friends were members, and the baby pool was our go-to place when our children were young. As they grew up, they participated in swim team, junior golf, and tennis. When my cousin Gloria Feld visited from Milwaukee one summer, we took her to Oakwood, where she caught the eye of lifeguard Jake Golding, whom she married a few years later.

Oakwood has given us so many memories to cherish: Bob's and my wedding dinner, Ryan's and Jill's bar and bat mitzvah parties, my father's 80th birthday, and Bob's parents' 40th anniversary. When our children got married, we hosted Ryan and Katie's rehearsal dinner at Oakwood. When Jill and Andrew got married at Oakwood in 2013, Bob was president of the board. Jill and her dad walked down the aisle to the Beatles song "In My Life," which begins with "There are places I remember." How perfect since she, too, grew up at Oakwood.

From left, Midge Grossman, Jean Zeldin, and Janet Zwillenberg—Jerome Grossman's wife and daughters—pay tribute to Jerome on his 80th birthday.

More recently, our grandchildren are enjoying fried chicken buffets and golfing with "Pops." We often have extended family gatherings at Oakwood for Rosh Hashanah and Thanksgiving. Even my Southwest High School class reunion is being held there, largely due to the club's beauty and its longtime reputation for excellent food and great service.

Much about Oakwood has changed over the decades. Older memories merge with new ones, reminding us how much Oakwood has enriched our family's life.

Addendum

OAKWOOD WOMENS GOLF CLUB CHAMPIONS

1915 Helen Griff	1922 Marguerite Levy	1947 Shirley Present
1917 Mrs. Sam Heilbrun	1923 Helen Griff Lyon	1948 Laveta Rubin
1918 Mrs. Sam Heilbrun	1924 Helen Griff Lyon	1949 Laveta Rubin
1919 Mrs. Sam Heilbrun	1927 Helen Griff Lyon	1950 Laveta Rubin
1921 Mrs. Sam Heilbrun	1939 Laveta Rubin	1951 Shirley Present

1952 Esther "Babe" Mallin	1971 Jean Nachman	1986 Laura Sechrist
1953 Betty Greenstein	1974 Cathy Stern	1987 Ellen Laner
1954 Betty Greenstein	1975 Cathy Stern	1988 Pat Morse
1955 Esther "Babe" Mallin	1976 Susan Kasle	1989 Leslie Herman
1956 Esther "Babe" Mallin	1977 Beverly Brick	1990 Leslie Herman
1957 Hortense Brozman	1978 Beverly Brick	1991 Lynn Poskin
1958 Shirley Present	1979 Beverly Brick	1992 Lynn Poskin
1959 Hortense Brozman	1980 Shirley Present	1993 Lynn Poskin
1960 Esther "Babe" Mallin	1981 Eileen Cohen	1994 Lynn Poskin
1961 Shirley Present	1982 Cathy Stern	1995 Leslie Herman
1962 Jean Nachman	1983 Cathy Stern	1998 Lynn Poskin
1963 Esther "Babe" Mallin	1984 Cathy Stern	1999 Lynn Poskin
1966 Hortense Brozman	1985 Barbara Laner	2000 Lynn Poskin
1970 Harriett Trepner		

2001 Barbara Hodes	2009 Amy Greif	2017 Lynn Poskin
2002 Phyllis Cohen	2010 Lynn Poskin	2018 Lynn Poskin
2003 Camille Reid	2011 Kay Johnson	2019 Meg Adkins
2004 Camille Reid	2012 Kay Johnson	2020 Meg Adkins
2005 Camille Reid	2013 Kay Johnson	2021 Lynn Poskin
2006 Lynn Poskin	2014 Lynn Poskin	2022 Meg Adkins
2007 Amy Greif	2015 Lynn Poskin	2023 Meg Adkins
2008 Amy Greif	2016 Lisa Block	

OAKWOOD MENS GOLF CLUB CHAMPIONS

1921 Sam Bren	1950 Leon Karosen	1962 Henry Present
1922 Bert Berkowitz	1951 Merrill Rose	1963 Arnold Garfinkel
1923 Sam Bren	1952 Fred Kornblum	1964 Arnold Garfinkel
1924 Martin Stein	1953 Berry Bird	1965 Arnold Garfinkel
1925 Eddie Guettel	1954 Henry Present	1966 Arnold Garfinkel
1926 Martin Stein	1955 Merrill Rose	1967 Leonard Rose
1927 Martin Stein	1956 Berry Bird	1968 Arnold Garfinkel
1931 Martin Stein	1957 Henry Present	1969 Leonard Rose
1934 Don Loeb	1958 Henry Present	1970 Bob Mallin
1940 Martin Stein	1959 Berry Bird	1971 Arnold Garfinkel
1947 Jack Printz	1960 Berry Bird	1972 Leonard Rose
1948 Henry Present	1961 Fred Kornblum	1973 Leonard Rose
1949 Merrill Rose		1974 Leonard Rose

1975 Arnold Garfinkel	1988 Mike Shteamer	2001 Greg Johnson
1976 Tom Sight	1989 Bert Benjamin	2002 Mike Shteamer
1977 Mike Shteamer	1990 Bert Benjamin	2003 Mike Shteamer
1978 Barton Cohen	1991 Barton Cohen	2004 Mike Shteamer
1979 Bert Benjamin	1992 Barton Cohen	2005 Matt Koenigsdorf
1980 Jack Brozman	1993 Keith Novorr	2006 Andy Epstein
1981 Jack Brozman	1994 Bert Benjamin	2007 Mike Shteamer
1982 Bert Benjamin	1995 Bert Benjamin	2008 Mike Shteamer
1983 Bert Benjamin	1996 Greg Johnson	2009 Greg Johnson
1984 Mike Shteamer	1997 Doug Wacker	2010 Greg Johnson
1985 Doug Stone	1998 Bert Benjamin	2011 Greg Johnson
1986 Bert Benjamin	1999 Bert Benjamin	2012 Matt Koenigsdorf
1987 Bert Benjamin	2000 Spence Fitzgibbons	2013 Greg Johnson

2014 Greg Johnson	2017 Mason Emmott	2020 Mike Ellis
2015 Greg Johnson	2018 Mason Emmott	2021 Curtis Yonke
2016 Mike Shteamer	2019 Mike Ellis	2022 Curtis Yonke
		2023 Curtis Yonke

* Except as expressly mentioned otherwise, all references to the golf course and record scores in this book are from the period before 2020 and do not take into account the changes that have occurred to the course since then. Oakwood's golf course has undergone extensive renovations since 2020 earning it top ratings for difficulty. Accordingly, record scores mentioned in this book are not deemed comparable to record scores set since 2020 such as the 66 set by Curtis Yonke since 2020 and broken by Chase Hanna with a 65 on April 17, 2024 or by future scores.

CLUB PRESIDENTS

1881–1884
B.A. Feineman

1884–1894
unknown

1895
Nathan Lorie

1896
Sol Block

1897–1898
Grant Rosenzweig

1899–1900
A. Judah

1901–1902
Sieg Harzfeld

1903–1904
Isaac Bachrach

1905–1906
Felix Kander

1907–1908
Alexander Rothenberg

1909–1911
A.C. Wurmser

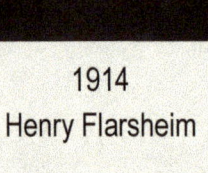

1912
Julius Lyons

1917
Morris Stern

1913
I.E. Bernheimer

1918
Lewis Oppenstein

1914
Henry Flarsheim

1915–1916
Alexander Rothenberg

1919–1920
Bernhard Adler

1921
Julius Lyons

1922–1923
E.B. Berkowitz

1924–1925
Walter Negbaur

1926
Lewis Oppenstein

1927
Sol Berkson

1928–1930
E.B. Berkowitz

1931–1932
Lester Siegel

1933–1935
George Oppenheimer

1936–1937
Paul Uhlmann, Sr.

1938–1940
E.B.Berkowitz

1941–1942
Charles Tucker

1943–1944
O.J. Printz, M.D.

1945–1946
Sidney Altschuler

1947–1948
Leon J. Meyer

1949–1950
Hy Davidson

1951–1952
Morris Shlensky

1953–1954
Harry Rubin

1959–1960
David (Tim) Blond

1955–1956
Joseph Printz, M.D.

1961–1962
Erwin R. Sackin

1957–1958
Paul Greenwood

1963–1964
Jacob Brown

1965
Adolph K. Scharff

1966–1967
Berry Bird

1968–1969
Jack Reitzes

1970–1973
Don Stein

1974–1975
William M. Klein

1976–1977
Henry Present

1978–1979
Leonard Rose

1985–1987
Bennett "Bud" Levy

1980–1981
Frank Hoffman

1988–1989
Melvin E. Krigel

1982–1984
Harold Tivol

1990–1991
Stanley Goldberg

1992–1993
Stanley H. House

1998–2000
Ward A. Katz

1994–1995
Irwin E. Blond

2001–2002
David Goodman

1996–1997
James Greenwood

2003–2004
Jeff Rosen

Oakwood Country Club

2005–2006
Jerry Miller

2012–2012
Bob Zeldin

2007–2008
Dr. Jeffrey Brick

2012–2014
Polly Kramer

2008–2010
Bill Koenigsdorf

2015–2016
Mike Fishman

2016–2017
Steve Katz, Bob Tucci & Bill Intrater,
Executive Committee

2017–2019
Lynn Poskin

2020–2021
Aaron March

CLUB MANAGERS

1910 Joseph Haar	1953 Leif Halvarsen	2010–2014 Chris Bancroft
1916–1926 Albert Lipper	1953–1969 Robert Benish	2014–2017 Dedra Rippee
1927–1940 Philip Daston	1969 Steve Pigg	2017 Michael Charest (interim)
1940– William Sommers	1970 Danny Villegas	2017–2021 Mark Maroon
1944– Paul Brantley	1970–1992 Hans Weyh	2021–2022 Brett Plymell
1944 Kenneth Erickson	1992–2001 Claudio Caviglia	2022– Steven Shrawder
1945–1951 Robert Benish	2001–2003 Gerald King	
1951 Alfred Addington	2003–2010 Kathy Brown	

HEAD GOLF PROFESSIONALS

1912 Arthur Boggs	1927–1932 Frank Madden	1997–2000 J.R. Rotarius
1913–1917 Jim "Skokie" Watson	1932–1942 Bunny Torpey*	2000–2006 Jimmy Farrell
1914–1916 Fred Clarkson	1945 R.E. "Bumps" Barnes	2007–2008 Troy Haltermann
1917 Cliff Booth	1945–1957 Bunny Torpey	2008–2015 Todd Stice
1918 Charles Bell	1958–1982 Herman Scharlau	2015–2017 Sean Daugherty
1919–1922 Louis Montressor	1882-1988 Billy Peterson	2018 Chris Bussell
1922–1927 Charlie Matthews	1988–1997 Bill Baraban	2018–2022 Randy Shade**
		2020–present Hunter Hayes

*Bunny Torpey was in the military service from 1/1/43–11/18/45. Torpey left in 1957 and was succeeded by Herman Scharlau in 1958.
** Randy Shade is Director of Golf and Hunter Hayes is Head Golf Professional, separate positions created since 2020.

CURRENT MEMBERS
At time of publication — April 2024

Joseph and Angela Accurso	Jay and Pamela Besheer	Jeffrey and Stephany Brick
Michael and Margaret Adkins	Steve and Jennifer Bessenbacher	Lynne Brown
Jeffrey and Cathy Alpert	Marty and Cheryl Bicknell	Norwood (Woody) and Jennifer Brown III
Jeffrey Anthony	Gene and Kelisen Binder	Jack and Fran Brozman
Tyler and Sarah Arens	Bruce and Suzi Blackman	Brennan and Lauren Burns
Nathan Arnell and Heidi Hellring	Kenneth and Lisa Block	Robert and Helen Bushman
Richard and Barbara Atlas	Suzy Block	Stephen Butler
Wayne and Lisa Auer	William Block	Craig and Fran Campbell
Terry and Zulema Bassham	Andrew Block	Andrew and Maggie Campbell
Ann Baum	David and Lynne Bock	Rachel Carpenter
Anthony Beaudette	Daniel and Ellen Bolen	Joseph and Dina Carr
Irv and Sue McCord Belzer	Dan and Lila Bortnick	Gray Carter
Bert and Janice Benjamin	Harry and Cheryl Bosley	Mike Casey and Cathy Phillips
Doloris Benjamin	Wendy Brand	Max Caylor
Eric Bens	Ellen Bresky	
Loren and Merilyn Berenbom	George and Leslie Brett	
Jeff and Jamie Berg	Jackson Brett and Monet Straub	*(continued on next page)*

Answers to golf quiz in introduction

Father-Son	Merrill Rose (father) — Leonard Rose (son)
Mother-Son	Kay Johnson — Greg Johnson
Mother-Son	Kay Johnson — Matt Koenigsdorf
Mother-Son	Hortense Brozman — Jack Brozman
Brothers	Greg Johnson — Matt Koenigsdorf
Brother-Sister	Andy Epstein — Lynn Poskin
Husband-Wife	Henry Present — Shirley Present
Grandmother-Grandson	Helen Griff — Bert Benjamin*

*Ellen Laner and Duncan Laner would be a good guess but Duncan never competed in a club championship match, either as an adult or a junior.

William Chase and Elisabeth (Betse) Gage
Pati Chasnoff
Connor Childress and Bailey Degnan
Kevin and Suzy Christian
James and Barbara Clancey
Michael and Morgan Clark
Mark and Gaye Cohen
Phyllis Cohen
Howard and Debra Cohen
David and Carolyn Cohen
Lena Price and Tom Cohen
Timothy (TJ) and Kristina Collins
Mary Ann Collins
Summer Cook
Blake Cooper
Steve and Erica Coppinger
Victor and Rita Cosentino
John and Christina Cottle
Mark Cowee
Dylan Crandall
Keith and Ginger Creel
Alex and Abigail Cuenca
Douglas and Pamela Curry
Nicholas Curry and Meghan Shirline
David and Jane Dalton
Quinn and Brooke Damon
Gregg Davidson and Sirenna Beyer
Lois Davidson

Michael and Amy Dempewolf
Sam Devinki and Mary Stahl
David and Erika Dickey
Anthony and Lillian Dona
William and Marilyn Dorzab
Michael and Beth Driks
Brett and Linda DuBay
Ian Edwards
Dennis Egan and Vicky Clayman
Michael and Jessica Ellis
Jon and Julia Ellis
Brenden and Nicole Allen Ellis
James Ellis
Brantley and Carol Elsberry
David and Amy Embry
David and Helen Emmott
Andrew and Anne Epstein
William and Jill Esry
Thomas Everitt
Brock and Savannah Falley
Michael and Ruth Fedotin
Brian and Catherine Fedotin
Joel Feigenbaum and Sharon Fate
Howard and Lisa Feingold
Paul Fingersh and Brenda Althouse
Michael and Marlene Fishman
Chip and Amy Fleischer
Sheldon and Cherie Fleishman
Chris Ford and Melissa Oliva
Floyd and Bari Freiden

Bradley and Theresa Freilich
David and Carol Ann Freirich
Frank and Sondra Friedman
William Fromm and Jackie Hadl Fromm
Dan and Kristen Fromm
Richard and Jeanne Galamba
Mark and Melinda Gammon
Bruce Garner
Michael Garry
David Garry
Joshua and Ronna Garry
Bill and Christena Gautreaux
Jeff and Polly Gentry
Donald and Lisa Gessen
James Getto and Kristen Korona
H. Lance Goldberg
Susan Goldsmith
Edward Goldstein and Rachel Krantz
David Goodman and Janis Rovick
Frank and Rachel Granatino
Trent and Julie Green
Lawrence Greenbaum and Song Yang
Frederick and Christina (Tina) Greenbaum
Laura Greenbaum
Aaron Greenbaum
Gabriel Greenbaum and Erin Thompson
Lee Greif and Amy Stepp Greif
Chad and Taylor Grossenkemper

Robert and Bette Grossman
Harvey and Patty Grossman
Michael and Rebecca Gude
Beau and Callie Hahn
Dayton (Buddy) and Debbie Hahs
Myron Haith and Linda Steeves Haith
Josh Haith
David and Claire Hall
Stephanie Harris
Dave and Susan Harris
Johnny and Susan Hart
Kurt and Christy Hartner
Bob and Devan Hartnett
Sudarshan Hebbar and Janet Mittenfeiner
Judith Helm
Barnett and Shirley Helzberg
Mathew and Lauren Hensley
Joseph and Cathy Hiersteiner
Peter and Jean Hill
Harry and Gail Himmelstein
John and Elizabeth Hjalmarson
JJ and Megan Hjalmarson
William and Mara Hodes
Robert and Judith Hoehn
Matthew and Claudia Hoffman
Mark Hogan
Alex (Rocky) and Susan Horowitz
Benjamin and Kelley Hotaling
Jeff and Jody House
Stanley and Emily House

Curt and Lauren Huston
Matthew and Janet Ida
Joseph and Hannah Ida
Lucas and Megan Ingala
William and Lynn Intrater
John and Jennifer Isenberg
Tom and Ann Isenberg
Jonathan Jacobs and Eli Bresky
Alan and Cynthia Jacobs
Andrew and Elizabeth Jacobs
Kenneth and Karen Jaggers
Jeff and Ilene Jerwick
Frederick Jiang and Jing Jin
Justin and Beverly Johl
Benjamin (Max) Johnson
Grant Jordan and Joan (Peg) Quinly
Jordan Jurcyk and Patrice Greenbaum
Rick and Pam Kahle
Charles and Judith Kahn
Theodore Kahn
Curtis Kaine and Emily Gray
Stephen and Susan Kaine
Harvey and Michele Kaplan
Peter and Tricia Katz
Stephen and Ellen Katz
Ward and Donna Katz
Ryan and Dana Katz
Randy and Molly Kellerman
James Kelly and Whitney Greaves

David Kiersznowski and Michelle Ladas
Allan King and Nancy Bean
Lloyd and Marie Kissick
James and Lisa Klein
Robert and Mary Knighton
Anthony and Sara Knipp
Gregg and Tammi Knipp
Joseph and Frances Knudson
Herbert and Nancy Kohn
Gregory and Meredith (Mimi) Kopulos
Tyler and Julie Korona
Tammy Kratzberg
William and Becky Krueger
Joel and Marcie Laner
Edward and Carol Lapin
Allen and Barbara Lefko
Bill and Randi Lefko
Lisa Lefkovitz
Jeffrey and Kristi Legette
Joel and Sandra Leibsohn
Nicole Levy
Beverly Lewis
Michael and Beth Liss
Marc and Jennifer Loe
Rodney and Shirley Loesch
Peter and Ann Long
William and Melisa Love
Glenn and Nicole Lowenstein
Eduardo and Georgina Luckie
Kyle and Maya Luke

Ryan and Shelby Luzenske
Zachary and Linsey Mallin
Thomas Mancuso
Aaron March
Mark and Cathy Maslan
Gregg Matson and Marilyn Moberg
Heath and Erica Mayor
Michael and Laurie Mazon
Jay McBride and Lucy Fitzpatrick
Thomas and Rebecca McCormack
Brian and Tangie McGlothen
Sarah McGreevy
Foss McKay
Shorty and Denise McKenny
Joe McKenny
Tim McQuaid and Mary Pat Shelledy
Don and Cindy Mead
Lance and Lissa Melber
Edward and Tess Merriman
James and Brenda Merryfield
Mark and Danielle Metz
Christopher and April Meyer
Jerry Jay and Lauren Miller
Tanner Miller and Jordan DeLeon
Lukas Miller
Kent and Cathy Misemer
Kama Moseley
James Mulhall
Matthew and Julie Mulhern
John and Diana Mullen

Mark Myron and Deborah Smith
Lewis and Susan Nerman
Greg and Ashley Nerman
Michael Norris and Sarah Tobaben
Keith and Vicki Novorr
Robert and Diane O'Byrne
Terrence and Nancy O'Neill
Patrick Orndoff
David and L. Suzanne Orscheln
Eric Orscheln
Patrick Ottensmeyer and Deanne Porter
Joe Pachman and Joan Hennessey
Steven and Karen Pack
Louis (Dee) and Joyce Pack
Zachary Pack
Mark and Colleen Patterson
Joel and Brenda Pelofsky
Lisa Pelofsky and Karen Mollus
Greg and Mickie Peppes
Robert Pirnie
David and Carol Porter
Joe and Lynn Poskin
Brady Poskin
Tommy and Lucy Dale Poskin
Kent and Andrea Price
Jeffrey and Reese Quibell
Michael and Kathleen Rainen
Sam and Lindsay Reagan
Gerald and Camille Reid
Grant Reves and Ashley Shores

Scott and Cindy Richey
Rick Roper
Jeffrey and Carole Rosen
Steven and Lisa Ruben
Nelson Sabatas, Jr.
Nelson and Rachel Sabates
Adam and Julana Sachs
Phil Saferstein
Daniel and Caroline Saferstein
Jonathan and Suzanne Saferstein
Steve Scanlon
Daniel and Miriam Scharf
William and Fani Schifman
Alex Schifman
Jeffrey and Amy Schmid
Alexander and Eden Schulte
Michael and Cathy Schultz
Mitchell and Brooke Schwartz
Frederic and Cathy Seligson
James Seward
Scott and Heather Shachtman
Peter and Amy Shapiro
David and Jill Shapiro
Matthew Shapiro
Justin and Meg Shaw
Jim and Stephanie Sheridan
Matthew Sheridan
Monica Shrawder
Michael Shteamer and Linda Jordan
Richard and Paula Shteamer

Lester and Myra Siegel
Bonnie and Matthew Siegel
Elaine Sight
Thomas Sight
Zachary and Ashley Sight
Eric Sildon and Lucy Shackelford
Michael Sinks
Ted and Pauline Sleder
David and Jacquelyn Smart, V
Kaleb Smith
Rusty and Angie Smith
Thomas and Teri Smith
Mike and Kathy Snyder
Gregg Soli
Victoria Sorrentino
Neil and Blanche Sosland
L. Josh and Jane Sosland
Daniel and Shari Spier
Jeff and Elizabeth Spivak
Daniel and Kristin Sprague
Bob and Cindy Steer
Carter Steer and Maura Kessler
Austin Steer
Howard Steinberg
Kyle Steinbrecher
Dan (John) and Jane (Mary) Stepp
Frank Sterneck
Robin Sterneck
Parker Sterneck
Phillip Stewart
Michael and Michella Stiles

Matt and Amy Streeter
Donald Swartz and Karen Glickstein
Steve and Evelina Swartzman
Brian and Niki Switzer
Joseph and Judi Tauber
Trevor and Lauren Taylor
Jason and Jessica Taylor
Robert and Crystal Taylor
Jeremy Terman and Katy Kenyon
Justin and Chandler Thompson
Mark Thornhill and Maria Donigan
Clifford and Carol Trenton
Steve and Debra Trenton
Robert and Cynthia Tucci
Robert and Stacie Turtledove
Patricia Uhlmann
Chris and Tracey Vaeth
Karthik Vamanan and Rashna Madan
Charles and Jennifer Vath
Kyle and Kassandra (Kasey) Vena
Robert (Bobby) and Clare Vickers, Jr.
James and Kathy Vigliaturo
Betsey Villarreal and Mike Arnold
John Wagner and Deborah Gifford
Joel Waldman and Annette Burnsides Waldman
Myron and Nicole Corbett Wang
John Ward, II
Peyton and Sophia Warwick

Hadley and Angie Warwick
Taylor and Taylor Warwick
Christian Wead and Kody Ross
Adam Weindling
Howard and Irene Weiner
Vance and Frances Wentz
David and Jennifer Wentz
Arica Westmeyer
Cameron Wilkerson
Douglas and Jane Willhoite
Michael Wilson and Jillian Collins
Sean Wirtz
Russell and Leslie Wismer
Steven and Kay Wolf
Robert and Marcia Wolff
Conner and Caitlin Wood
Dennis and Julie Wood
Curtis and Lauren Yonke
Bryan and Susan Yourdon
David and Linda Zachariah
Kristopher and Lindsey Zeid
Robert and Jean Zeldin
Paul Zenk and Kathleen Weatherstone

The accuracy of the names of the members including the surnames used by spouses or partners of members is based upon club records and reasonable verification efforts.

THEN AND NOW

THEN AND NOW

THEN AND NOW

THEN AND NOW

THEN AND NOW

THEN AND NOW

www.ingramcontent.com/pod-product-compliance
Lightning Source LLC
Chambersburg PA
CBHW062023050526

44107CB00106B/1012